Every One You Teach

Practical Strategies That Value Each Student

**by Rosann Englebretson
and Marlene LeFever
with Steve Wamberg**

Suggested Ways to Use This Book

- **If you are a Sunday school teacher:**
  Read the Introduction and Chapters 1 and 2. Skim Chapter 3 and read the parts that apply to your class. Then find and read the age-level chapter that matches your students.

- **If you oversee a Christian Education program:**
  Read the book from beginning to end to get a comprehensive understanding of how students learn and how to help teachers teach those students effectively.

- **If you are leading a teacher-training session:**
  Give copies of the book to your teachers and ask them to read the Introduction and Chapters 1–3 ahead of time. Discuss chapters 1–3 as a whole group. Then divide into age-level groups to study the appropriate age-level chapters. Come back together as a group and use the Epilogue as an affirming, inspirational closing.

- **If you want a practical Christian Education resource:**
  Keep this helpful handbook in plain sight—and consult it often!

Reach Every One You Teach:
Practical Strategies That Value Each Student

Cover design by Image Studios
Printed in the U.S.A.

Contents

Symbols Used in This Book

 Points to an interesting quote that will probably stretch your thinking.

 Take 3 minutes to think about a question or two that will help you apply the material you've just read to your unique situation.

 Take a couple of minutes to review the chapter.

 A helpful list of do's and don'ts that describe what works and what doesn't with certain age qroups.

 A list of short questions to help you evaluate the effectiveness of the curriculum you're now using.

Introduction

Congratulations!
Your Reach Goes Way
Beyond Your Grasp!

The sun danced through the stained glass into the sanctuary. It was a gorgeous spring day—just right for the first Sunday in June. Laura Phelps watched with pride as Tommy Sutterlin walked to the podium to receive a gift from the church for his graduation.

"Tommy Sutterlin," the minister intoned. "Honor society, citizenship award, four-year cross-country and track letterman, president of the Paynesville Fellowship of Christian Athletes chapter." The congregation applauded. "Here's your Study Bible, son. Congratulations!"

Tommy took the Bible and set it on the podium. The minister continued, "And Tommy has asked to make a presentation of his own today."

Tommy took a small box from behind the podium and held it up for the congregation to see. "This is my citizenship award from school. I want to share it with you all. I know you all took a special interest in me when my family wasn't doing so well. The way things were four years ago, it would have been easier for me to imagine myself in a detention center than ever graduating from high school. But you helped change that.

"I would especially like to thank Mrs. Phelps, my Sunday school teacher, who took the time to explain God's Word so I could

understand it. I'd like her to come up now to receive this award on behalf of all of you in the church."

Laura was overwhelmed for a moment, but she finally made it to the podium to receive the small box from Tommy. She was speechless, and could only hug Tommy through her tears.

The feeling lasted through the service straight into the family car on the way home after the service. Laura's husband playfully asked, "So, still planning to give up teaching Sunday school?"

Everyone who has ever taught a Bible class prays for the kind of payoff that Laura Phelps received. The medal doesn't matter. But to see a student growing in Christ does.

If you picked up this book, you're probably involved somehow in Christian education. If you are a Sunday school teacher, then that makes you a member of one of the largest volunteer forces in North America—a force 4 million strong, all engaged in the effort to make God's Word understandable to over 30 million students every week.

As a Sunday school teacher, your reach already extends beyond your grasp. The smile that settles an uncomfortable student, your efforts to include every student in the learning process—these all add up to help your students catch a glimpse of what God is like.

"Hold on," you might say. "I *try* to make every session connect with every student. But I still don't feel like it's working. I still get my share of blank stares and silence during class. Reaching *every* one I teach? Each Sunday? Sounds impossible."

It isn't.

The Good, the Better, and the Bottom Line

Doing your best for your Sunday school class involves three things: the *ability* to help students discover God's truth for themselves (your God-given giftedness), the amount of *time* you have to prepare and teach, and the *resources* that are available to you. *One of the resources* that can have a significant impact on your effectiveness in the classroom is *the curriculum* you use.

Have you had a chance to take a hard look at your curriculum? Have you checked it over to find out how well it connects with your students? We recently checked out several popular curricula to see how they fared.

The *good* news was that the basic plan of most of them—the strategy behind the educational, spiritual, and interactive parts of the curriculum—was sound.

The *better* news was that there were things that could be done to make curriculum work even more effectively for students like yours. Like you, we've noticed the blank stares and silence that sometimes met our approach in the classroom. Those were often painful and discouraging experiences for us. There had to be a way to reach those students we seemed to be missing.

We sensed it might be time for some changes. So we sought out ways to shape a curriculum that could reach this generation of students right where they are—in your classroom. These adjustments were based on proven methods that gave a fresh approach to educational and developmental ideas that have stood the test of time.

The *bottom line* was that adjustments were needed in two general categories:

(1) the natural learning cycle; and

(2) age grouping.

The "why" and "how" of these adjustments make up the majority of this book.

Has the pace of change accelerated beyond your comfort zone? Are the rules that guided your decisions in the past no longer reliable? If so, you are just like everyone else who is paying attention. You're not imagining things.
— Stan Davis & Christopher Meyer

The Heart of Change

Our motivation for suggesting changes in curriculum is the same thing that motivates you as a teacher: doing what is best for your students.

If we hesitate to change, it might seem like we were more concerned with maintaining a few traditional approaches to Sunday school than the way those methods affected the ones we serve. But if our purpose is to first serve Christ, and then our students, we have to be willing to make adjustments.

What classroom or curriculum changes would have most benefited your experience as a Sunday school student? How about as a Sunday school teacher?

In the pages that follow, you'll encounter many time-tested ideas for change. Compare the principles presented in this book with the curriculum you're now using. Are the resources you're using serving your needs? Do they give ideas that will reach *all* of the students in your class, or just some? Making adjustments can be difficult, but our hope and prayer for you is that this book will help the transition go a little more smoothly.

So enjoy your journey through the pages that follow. We're about to show you . . .

- why Christian education is so critical in the advancement of God's Kingdom;
- crucial learning styles that characterize every student you teach;
- the reasons to rethink the ways kids are grouped in your Sunday school;
- the learning characteristics of each age group; and
- how to make your classroom a place where every student succeeds in learning God's Word.

If you're part of your church's Christian education ministry, you're already touching lives in eternally significant ways. Is your heart's desire to have an even greater impact—to reach *every* student your teach? If so, read on. This book was written for you.

Chapter 1

Why Sunday School Matters

You may be familiar with the current statistics on Sunday school. We've already mentioned that there are over 4 million Sunday school teachers reaching over 30 million students today.

Most of that teaching force is made up of dedicated volunteers. Stop and think just for a moment: What other organizations have that many weekly volunteers? With that kind of commitment from that many people, Sunday school teachers could change the world . . . couldn't they?

Well, to God's glory, that's our goal.

A Quick History of Sunday School

Religious education, particularly of children, has always been the responsibility of God's people. This mandate is summed up by Moses, speaking to God's people:

These are the commands, decrees and laws the LORD your God directed me to teach you to observe in the land that you are crossing the Jordan to possess, so that you, your children and their children after them may fear the LORD your God as long as you live by keeping all his decrees and commands that I give you, and so that you may enjoy long life. Hear, O Israel, and be careful to obey so that it may go well with you and that you may increase greatly in a land flowing with milk and honey, just as the LORD, the God of your fathers, promised you.

*Hear, O Israel: The LORD our God, the LORD is one. Love the
LORD your God with all your heart and with all your soul and with
all your strength. These commandments that I give you today are to
be upon your hearts. Impress them on your children. Talk about
them when you sit at home and when you walk along the road, when
you lie down and when you get up. Tie them as symbols on your
hands and bind them on your foreheads. Write them on the door-
frames of your houses and on your gates (Deuteronomy 6:1-9).*

The command is clear: God's people are to keep His Word
before their children. This theme continues in the Psalms, as shown
in this example of a hymn sung at a religious festival:

> *Walk about Zion, go around her, count her towers,*
> *Consider well her ramparts, view her citadels,*
> > *that you may tell of them to the next generation.*
> > > *(Psalm 48:12-13)*

There's that idea again: teaching the next generation about the
ways of God. For thousands of years, the teaching of the next generation took place in families and local synagogues and churches.
Significant revivals throughout Church history brought with them a
renewed interest in God's Word. Religious education was continu-
ally rediscovered as a vital part of a child's training—and also as an
introduction to Christianity for those outside the faith.

Sunday school, as we have come to know it, began as a
concerted effort in eighteenth-century England. The "charity school
movement," as it was known then, provided an alternative school for
child laborers of the Industrial Revolution who worked through the
week. The program provided basic training in reading, writing, arith-
metic, and spiritual training as chosen by a local sponsor—which
was almost always a church.

That same model was adopted in the American colonies and the
young United States for children on the streets and across the fron-
tier. This model became the pattern for the United States' public
school systems. In 1824 the American Sunday School Union, based
in Philadelphia, was working in cities in the eastern United States.
This association eventually moved throughout the Mississippi
Valley providing basic education and spiritual training.

After a while, five-day-a-week common or "public" schools began to emerge on the scene. Because the First Amendment forbade preference for one church over another in the states, the spiritual training of public schools was based on those elements of Christianity that could be held as "common." Sunday schools then became more focused on specific doctrinal Christian teaching within local churches. Families looking for a strong theological emphasis looked to Sunday schools to complement the public schools (Kennedy 1966).

Do the families of your Sunday school students have any expectations of you as a teacher? If so, what do you think they are?

This pattern, established nearly a century and a half ago, has lasted to this day for most families and churches in the United States. Families look to Sunday schools to complement their children's weekday education. In fact, Sunday school is a place that many parents and students expect an intelligent response to the faith challenges that students encounter in some public schools.

Fifteen-year-old Andrew is an honors student. He could graduate from high school a year ahead of his class if he wanted to. He participates in Sunday school, and sometimes shows flashes of interest. But he stays quiet most of the time.

That's why Jeff, his Sunday school teacher, was surprised that Andrew stayed around after class one Sunday.

"Jeff," Andrew said, "I have a question."

Oh boy, *Jeff thought.* Am I going to be able to handle his question? *"What's up, Andrew?"*

"My advanced placement biology teacher keeps hammering me about evolution."

"What's the issue?"

"Same old stuff. God's a myth. Darwin is God. How can I get him off my case?"

> *"Let's see—God's a myth, Darwin is God . . . so that makes Darwin a myth?"*
>
> *Andrew grinned. "I've gotta remember that one. Look, we always get to the point of 'first cause' and then he gives up. I'm getting tired of it week after week."*
>
> *"Do you want to pray about it?"*
>
> *"Sure. But after we pray, could you help me come up with some solid answers?"*

Andrew and Jeff have worked out the kind of relationship that demonstrates some of the best that Sunday school can offer: trust, guidance, challenges that produce growth. These all fall into line with the classic purposes of Christian education.

 When your students are working through a fairly complex issue, how do you usually respond? What kind of help do they need from you at this stage of life?

Why We Bother with Christian Education

> *"Roger, it's time to get up."*
>
> *A groan comes from under the covers. "Ugh. Let me sleep."*
>
> *"Roger, you need to get ready for Sunday school."*
>
> *Another groan. "Aw, it's so boring. Why do I have to go to Sunday school anyway?"*
>
> *"Because, Roger, <u>you're the teacher</u>."*

Let's face it. There are Sundays when we feel just like Roger. We wake up asking, "Why do we have Sunday school anyway?" And *we're the teachers.*

So let's review four major reasons for Sunday school. You'll probably think of more, but these cover a lot of territory.

Reason 1: Sunday school can be a place where people meet Jesus Christ. This opportunity is often overlooked, but it shouldn't be. Think of the number of children, for instance, who come to

Sunday school but never stick around for the church service where the Gospel is preached. Think of the number of teenagers who sit in the back of the church bored to tears, but who make it to Sunday school because in class you give them a chance to talk about what they think. Consider the adults who feel that the sermons go way over their heads, but who keep coming to Sunday school to learn more about God with their friends.

People can be exposed to the Gospel in a variety of ways as they participate in the church. Sunday school should be one of those places. Your classroom can be a place where students have the regular opportunity to encounter—and accept—Christ as their own Savior.

Reason 2: Sunday school can teach people how to become contributing members of the Christian community. Sunday school can help people sort through the issues that face Christians today—and suggest actions that can be taken in response to those issues. Sunday school can help people understand some of the practical implications of the Christian faith. This time of teaching can help explain sound Christian doctrine and clarify solid biblical ethics. These are all lofty objectives, to be sure. But Sunday school remains uniquely positioned to address each one of them.

Reason 3: Sunday school can help students appropriate their Christian heritage. The Christian heritage is anything but mysterious. The legacy of our faith is built upon specific people at specific points in history. Our heritage stems from inspired written documents which have been gathered together as the sacred Scriptures. Sunday school presents a singular opportunity to offer this rich heritage to those we teach.

Reason 4: Sunday school can be a training ground for students to fulfill the Christian mission. A Sunday school class can be a strategic force in helping students put their faith into action in their everyday lives. This time with your students can be a place where day-to-day strategies are generated. Students can lovingly hold one another accountable for the commitments they make during their time together. They can keep one another in prayer, and share regular updates on how their faith out of the classroom is working. They can think and pray together on how best to implement what they believe at home, in school, and on the job. Sunday school is a fantastic place to transform tentative Christians into enthusiastic workers for the Kingdom of God (Shinn, 1966).

No great nation can ever survive its own temptations and its own follies that does not indoctrinate its children in the Word of God. . . . Every Sunday School should be a place where this great book is not only opened, is not only studied, is not only revered, but is drunk as if it were a fountain of life, is used as if it were the only source of inspiration and of guidance. — Woodrow Wilson

Where We're Going from Here

Now you've read a bit about the history of Sunday school. You've reviewed a few of the many reasons that Sunday school is a valuable tool in God's Kingdom. So without further delay, please proceed to the chapters that follow. In these pages, you'll encounter practical ways to make the most of every classroom session—and how to reach *every* student God gave you to teach.

There are at least four main reasons to encourage excellence in Sunday school:

Reason 1: Sunday school can be a place where people meet Jesus Christ.

Reason 2: Sunday school can teach people how to become contributing members of the Christian community.

Reason 3: Sunday school can help students appropriate their Christian heritage.

Reason 4: Sunday school can be a training ground for students to fulfill the Christian mission.

Chapter 2

The Best Way to Learn Is Naturally

Every person involved in putting this book together has had front-line experience in Christian education. Marlene remembers one very special Sunday school student:

Jeffrey arrived. Within 15 minutes, he had his teacher wishing she had called in sick with the measles. He drew fancy designs all over other kids' masterpieces. He used his chair as a launching pad. He found a Styrofoam cup and tore it into little pieces and began chewing them. "If you don't settle down," the teacher warned, "I'll send someone to get your father out of his class."

Jeffrey stopped and spit out the mushy Styrofoam so he could answer. "He doesn't go to church. I rode my bike here. I'm here by myself."

Weeks passed. Several of us taught Jeffrey's class. Once he realized what Sunday school was all about, he stopped eating strange substances and launching flying objects at moving kid-targets. Instead, he paid attention. He participated. He was enjoying himself and obviously happy to be in Sunday school.

Then one Sunday, he decided to try the worship service. He looked around the congregation, picked out the first person he recognized—me—and pushed through the row to plop his nine-year-old self between my husband and me.

I pointed to the page number of the next song in the bulletin. "Hey," he whispered loud enough to turn heads, "what is that thing?"

I explained that it was a worship guide. "Lemme see." He grabbed it and started reading. On the back page was a listing of the events for the week: Elders Prayer Group, Home Bible Study Group Leaders Meeting, Ladies Bible Study, and even Alcoholics Anonymous.

"Wow!" Jeffrey pointed to the list. "This is great. Can I come to all these? Are they fun like Sunday school?"

Don't you want all the Jeffreys we teach to be so excited about Sunday school that they can't conceive of anything that happens in the church being dull? We can start by using a teaching approach that reaches every one of our students. We call this approach the Natural Learning Cycle.

Around the Cycle

Researchers have discovered overwhelming evidence that following a specific teaching sequence results in the most effective learning. As Christians, we don't see this as an accident. Rather, it is evidence of a deliberate pattern that God has built into every human being. When we use this Natural Learning Cycle, we not only help our students learn and apply God's truth, but we also reach the different types of learners whom God brings into our classes.

Every student has a favorite step in the Natural Learning Cycle; at some point in the lesson, every student will have a chance to shine. In that favorite step, the student can take some peer leadership and be honored by you and the rest of the students. When a student knows that every lesson includes her smart step, she is willing to participate in all four steps in the Natural Learning Cycle. After all, her time is coming! She doesn't mind allowing others their minutes in the spotlight.

Step 1 of the Natural Learning Cycle: Motivating Your Students

Jeffrey didn't come to Sunday school in a vacuum. He brought his week along with him. He brought to class his feeling smart over his good grades this report period. With him came his dislike for broccoli. And he didn't leave his pain at home either. He still hurt because Ken showed him the birthday present he'd bought for his mom—and Jeffrey has no mother at home. These and hundreds of other details are near the surface of his mind. Unless his teacher is able to gather Jeffrey's thoughts and point them toward what he needs to learn about Jesus this week, he will not connect with God's Word.

A teacher following the Natural Learning Cycle starts by encouraging students to use their own interests and life experiences to focus on the Bible topic. The teacher's role in Step 1 is that of a *motivator.* Here, the job is to help students somehow move—often through talking, sharing, or even playing—from their lives outside class into some understanding that they need what the lesson will present.

For example, if the lesson focus is on Jesus' love, a teacher might start with pantomimes where Jeffrey and his friends silently act out what a world without love would be like. Then, together they discuss what was silently dramatized. Jeffrey brings his life experiences into class. Now he's focused on love, and his life experiences involving that act of the will. Now he's ready to study about God's love.

If the Bible story is about Thomas, who doubted that Jesus was alive after the crucifixion, Jeffrey's teacher might read statements that the students could either believe or doubt. Jeffrey and his friends would go to one side of the room if they believed the statement, and to the other side of the room if they doubted it. Then the kids could be encouraged to talk about other things they have trouble believing. When Jeffrey's mind is focused on doubts that kids his age have, his interest will be on the Bible and not Styrofoam snacks.

In Step 1 of the Natural Learning Cycle moves Jeffrey, (and all the children in the class), from being a discipline problem to being a boy who knows this lesson is specifically for him. He wants to find out more.

Some students, often called *Imaginative Learners,* prefer this step over any other because it best matches their preferred learning style. These students love to share ideas and listen to other people's ideas. Their self-identity sometimes depends on the number of friends they have. They want to make everyone feel welcome and part of the group. Their example can help the teacher set a positive tone for the whole class session.

A learning *style* is the way in which a person sees or perceives things best and then processes or uses what has been seen. Each person's learning style is as unique as a signature. When a person has something difficult to learn, that student learns faster and enjoys learning more if his or her unique learning style is affirmed by the way the teacher teaches. (LeFever 1994)

(For a comprehensive look at learning styles, check into Marlene LeFever's book *Learning Styles: Reaching Everyone God Gave You to Teach.*)

Step 2 of the Natural Learning Cycle: Informing Your Students

Into the Bible! This important step of the Natural Learning Cycle would never have captured Jeffrey's attention if his teacher had simply announced at the start of class, "Today I'm going to tell you the story of Thomas," or "Let's read these verses about how very much Jesus loves you." Jeffrey would have been more likely to build a mini-sculpture with his wad of chewing gum than to pay attention.

But he was prepared by Step 1, his interest captured. He'll keep his gum in his mouth and chew on God's Word at the same time.

During the second step of the Natural Learning Cycle, Jeffrey is learning more about the Bible itself. He's getting smarter about the facts in God's Word. He's starting to understand it. He's beginning to see that he can study it for himself. It's not just a book for Sunday school. It's a book he can read and think about at home.

In Step 2, the teacher becomes an *information giver* who makes sure students know what the Bible says. Sometimes she'll share what the students need to know. Other times she'll teach the students how to study for themselves, at their own age level, in ways that will stretch them.

About 30% of the students you teach will feel most at home in this step because it best matches the way they like to learn. They're often called *Analytic Learners*. They love facts, answering questions, and methods with measurable right answers. They want to hear new content every lesson, and as they get older, love dealing with ideas and concepts. The Imaginative Learners helped these students understand that the day's lesson is for them. The Analytic Learners will help the other students get involved with the lesson content.

Teachers often gravitate toward Analytical Learners because they love to learn in more school-like ways. Therefore, they don't usually present much of a discipline problem. How do you feel about them? How do you feel about the other 70% of your students?

Step 3 of the Natural Learning Cycle: Coaching Your Students

Welcome to the laboratory! In this step, Jeffrey practices using what he has learned in the Bible. How does it work? Is it more than words in a big book? Does it make sense to him? If kids his age really believe what they studied in the Bible, how must their lives change?

Not everyone practices in the same way. Some need to see what they have learned and process it through puzzles and word games. Others need to act out what might happen if they took what they have learned into their school or shared it with their friends. Some need to translate what they have learned into a project that will serve as a reminder of what they have learned.

In Step 3, a teacher takes on the role of *coach.* You'll help each student answer the question, "How can I put what I learned from today's lesson into practice?" You'll coach the students to practice ways to use what they learned this week through a variety of age-appropriate activities.

Choice in the laboratory is important! So is the laboratory's atmosphere. Keep it warm, personal, energetic, physical, and peer-centered.

When children have choices, their attention span is hooked from 10 to 90 minutes. When children are directed 100 percent of the time with no input from them, they will experience apathy and resentment, and their attention span will last for 10 minutes or less. (Jensen 1998)

You'll notice that some of your students prefer this step of the Learning Cycle over others. Sometimes these students are called *Common Sense Learners.* They'll want to take the facts and conduct a practical experiment to answer the question, "How does this work?"

Common Sense Learners benefit from the other students in the class to get them to this point in the lesson. They'll shine in this step as they help other students discover how the Bible truths of the lesson work today and why these truths make sense.

Because teachers are perpetual learners, they also have a preferred style of learning. That means they will intrinsically prefer one step of the Learning Cycle over the other three. As you teach, make sure you give all four steps of the Natural Learning Cycle equal time to make sure that every student has a chance to shine at some point in the lesson.

Step 4 of the Natural Learning Cycle:
Encouraging Your Students

This final step of the Natural Learning Cycle encourages Jeffrey to take on a homework assignment. And often that assignment isn't something the teacher suggests. It's something Jeffrey comes up with because he believes it's what Jesus is asking him to do. Yes! Really! His homework encourages him to live what he's learned from the Bible, the things he's practiced in the safety of the Sunday school laboratory.

Of course we never, ever call it "homework." Instead, it's a "life response." It's "living the Bible." It's "taking Jesus into my home." But, it's never, ever "homework!"

Monday may be the most important day of the Sunday school week. If a person doesn't put what has been learned into practice in the first 24 hours after learning it, the new knowledge will be lost.

Step 4 of the Natural Learning Cycle can be very creative. Sometimes Jeffrey's teacher will give him ideas for living what he's learned. Most of the time, she will point him in a general direction and encourage him to come up with his own ideas. The commitments he picks himself are usually much harder than anything the teacher would dare to assign.

"I will go all week without sassing my dad. Hey, he won't know what hit him." "I'll tell my friend about Jesus and ask him if he wants to bike to Sunday school with me next week."

Students who prefer this step in the Learning Cycle are often called *Dynamic Learners.* They enjoy coming up with ways to use what they have learned in the classroom during the week outside the classroom. They'll have exciting—perhaps even off-the-wall—ideas about how to make lesson content come alive in the week to come. They can get everyone excited about living the Christian life on Monday.

Teachers take on the role of *encourager* in Step 4 of the Learning Cycle. Here, a teacher assists the students in planning what they'll do for Jesus during the week. She evaluates their ideas, offering correction or expansion as needed. She encourages them in their attempts to put their ideas into action.

This is the most dangerous, but most exciting, part of the Natural Learning Cycle. Being a Christian isn't easy. Being more like Jesus this week than he was last week will be hard for Jeffrey. But until students have decided to live what they have learned, they may have had a fun time in class, but they haven't moved ahead in their Christian lives.

MENTAL FLEX

In his popular children's series *The Chronicles of Narnia*, C. S. Lewis uses the lion Aslan to represent Jesus. In one of the stories, the children who think the lion will be sweet and cuddly are warned, "He is not a tame lion."

The same thing should be said about Sunday school, where we learn about Jesus. It's not always predictably tame, sweet, cute, or comfortable. It's a place to practice what the Christian life is all about. The Christian life is not tame. It's not always safe. Picture Jeffrey living for Jesus at school. Picture Jeffrey sharing his Jesus-love with adults who think Jesus is just one of many spiritual choices. He could take some heat. Sunday school, real Sunday school, helps prepare him for these challenges.

The Natural Learning Cycle works with every age level, not just Jeffrey's elementary class. For example, an adult class in Woodstock, Georgia was studying Christian responses to anger. They wrote appropriate Scriptures on notecards to help them in the weeks ahead. Such a small assignment, but two months after that Sunday one of the members said, "My very angry friend called me. She was yelling so loud that I'm not sure she needed the phone. I pulled my anger cards from my purse and used them to calm her down. I helped her see the situation from God's eyes. What I learned in class is getting spread out to all of my friends."

In another adult class, the lesson was on witnessing. Josie, a new Christian, once had a bad reputation around town—drugs, alcohol abuse, you name it, and she had dabbled in it. But she was a Christian now. She was determined to put Step 4 of the Natural Learning Cycle into practice. Monday after the lesson, she created a big poster and put it in her clunker car's window telling her old friends that Christ made a difference in her life.

Learning Styles researcher Bernice McCarthy suggests that teachers can think of the Natural Learning Cycle as a clock. Students really haven't learned, she points out, until minute 59 on that clock—because that's when they agree to put what they've studied into practice.

There's More to This Cycle . . .

The Natural Learning Cycle is a great pattern that every teacher can successfully use. Discipline problems diminish because students are involved. Students learn because they are interested in the subject. Students are challenged to put what they learned into practice. Before the lesson begins, the teacher can ask students to talk about how they put their Step 4 plans into action the previous week. After every one has debriefed, a new cycle begins.

The Natural Learning Cycle encourages students to flex their minds and learn the way God made them—not the way people used to think He made them, and not even the way we might wish He had made them. The Natural Learning Cycle honors everyone God brings into our classrooms. We're not just teaching students who learn in the predictable school way.

We're teaching *every* one.

The Natural Learning Cycle is a proven pattern that can help every teacher reach every student in the classroom. The Cycle is described in four steps:

Step 1 captures a student's interest in the topic. Here the teacher is *a motivator* who helps students understand their need for the lesson. *Imaginative Learners* are the students who will best respond to this step, because they love to open up and to help others share too.

Step 2 helps students expand their understanding of the Bible. Here, the teacher is *an information giver* who offers the lesson content in age-appropriate ways. *Analytic Learners*, who love facts, ideas and questions, are the students who like this step best.

Step 3 allows students to practice the Bible lesson in the safety of the classroom. The teacher becomes *a coach* who helps students put the Bible lesson into action. *Common Sense Learners*—the students who thrive on action and high-touch learning—like this step best.

Step 4 sends the students home to live what they learned. The teacher's role here is that of *an encourager* who helps students evaluate their ideas about how they'll apply the lesson to their lives that week. Students who love experimenting with new ideas are often called *Dynamic Learners*. They'll like this final step the best.

If you'd like to see the Natural Learning Cycle in action, turn to the appendix on page 133.

Chapter 3

Reaching Students through Age Grouping

In an ideal world, we would match every student with a teacher. That's the best way to learn: one-on-one. Reality dictates, however, that we put groups of children together with one or two teachers. In this situation, the best way to group children is by single age level. But reality refines our vision again: in most of our churches, we simply cannot have a dedicated single-age class of children. So we must follow a workable strategy of age grouping.

This chapter outlines a strategy that focuses on age grouping for children. (There are grouping options for adults in Chapter 11 which is focused on teaching adults.) By the end of this chapter, you'll understand why *the way children think and learn* can be the most effective guideline to determine *the way we group children* in Sunday school.

Why Age Grouping Matters

One of the first requirements of effective teaching is that the teacher understand how students think and how they view the world. There are certain ages at which children simply do not have "what it takes" to learn certain things. It won't matter how well or how long those things are taught; some concepts are simply beyond the grasp of some students because of developmental reasons. That's why any effective teaching strategy must take into account students' ages and stages of development (Slavin 1994).

For example: An infant cannot tie a shoe. A two year old cannot read. A six year old cannot understand, much less explain, a metaphor. An adolescent cannot ignore what his peers think.

But sometimes we expect students to do things that are beyond their capacities. A good strategy of age grouping can help prevent that.

A Look at Traditional Age Groupings

Traditionally, Sunday schools grouped children as follows:

Age or Grade	*Grouping*
Birth through two	*Nursery*
Three through five year olds	*Preschool – Kindergarten*
1st and 2nd graders	*Primary*
3rd and 4th graders	*Middler*
5th and 6th graders	*Junior*
7th and 8th graders	*Junior High*
9th through 12th graders	*Senior High*

These groupings served the church well for some years. But upon closer examination, it's been discovered that these groupings don't always meet the developmental needs of the children we teach. Let's consider the stories of a few children to illustrate.

Joey: The Self-Contained Two Year Old

Joey is into everything. He learns through all five of his senses. He's "self-contained." He's not being "bad" when he wreaks havoc in his twos-and-threes Sunday school; *he's just being two years old.*

Three year olds actually enjoy doing things in groups. Two year olds can hardly stand groups. If you watch two year olds closely, you may notice them playing *next to* each other, but you're not likely to see them playing *with* each other. Their pretend play is usually solitary until age three (Schickedanz, et al, 1990). So the "herd" approach that can succeed with three year olds is destined to fail with two year olds. The concepts of cooperation and sharing simply haven't entered the two year old's mind (Ames, et al, 1979). Even the crayons and stickers that delight a three year old can be so challenging to the undeveloped small muscle skills of a two year old that they are simply a source of frustration—or a snack—to a child like Joey (Schickedanz, et al, 1990). In addition, two year olds are seldom toilet-trained as are their three-year-old counterparts. And two year olds use their senses to think. They explore the world through direct touch, taste, sight, hearing, and smell. In contrast, three year olds no longer have to touch something to know it exists (Ames, et al, 1979).

The results? Joey's teacher is frustrated from having to spend so much energy to keep Joey "in line" with the three year olds. Joey doesn't feel connected with the learning environment. He's not learning anything. He's being tolerated until he turns three and can "get with the program."

What if Joey was included with the toddlers for another year? It would mean restructuring traditional age groupings in his Sunday school. But the classroom benefits could far outweigh that temporary inconvenience (Video 1998).

Our suggestion here: *Group toddlers and twos together,* and put the threes, fours, and preschool fives together. You'll still maintain two groupings of preschool children, and that simple shift will probably ease a great deal of frustration for children and teachers alike.

The "new" preschool class of threes, fours and fives will enjoy group activities. They'll love the activities that challenge their small and large muscle skills. They'll begin to discuss the stories the teachers tell them—all activities that are beyond the capacity of two year olds.

Danielle: The Six-Year-Old Early Reader

Danielle is a charming first grader. She's six years old and learning to read. She's proud of the words she's mastered, and is constantly affirmed about her progress in school.

But in Sunday school, she's grouped with second graders. Her progress in reading is never fast enough for her second-grade classmates. No matter how hard she tries, they seem bored when she reads aloud. The printed material in class has too many words. She feels left behind.

Again, *when the learning environment doesn't fit the student, the student can be left out of the learning.* Danielle knows it's important to learn more about Jesus, but the class session is simply over her head (Video 1998).

Learning to read is the all-consuming task for kindergartners and first graders. Kindergarten used to be incidental in public education; now it's the norm for most children. Kindergarten has also made a shift from being a largely social experience to gaining an academic focus. In some school districts, in fact, kindergarten programs are now quite similar to what first grades once were (Slavin 1994).

The similarities between kindergarten and first grade are far greater than those between first grade and second grade. Five and ·six year olds are just learning to read. They've refined their large muscle and finger dexterity skills.

But five and six year olds haven't taken the step into the type of thinking where facts rule the day, as they do in the world of second graders. Seven year olds, who generally have taken that step, will begin to make distinctions between the real and the imaginary that are beyond their younger counterparts (Schickedanz, et al, 1990).

Perhaps even more problematic in grouping first and second graders together is the huge reading disparity between the two groups. This is certainly a significant frustration for children like Danielle. (There are always exceptions whenever abilities are addressed. But generally, the disparity is far more evident between first and second graders than between second and third graders.) Creating student material that meets both first and second graders "where they are" is a very difficult task. Usually, if the material is accessible to first graders, it is too easy for second graders. Or, if it's produced at a second grader reading level, it's too difficult for a new reader (Englebretson, et al, 1997).

Our suggestion for age groupings, then, is to group children with those who best align with their own development. *That would mean putting kindergartners and first graders together*, and *placing second and third graders together.*

The second- and third-grade class could enjoy material that better challenges their reading skills. They can handle series of instructions that would be daunting to first graders. They can reason in simple logical steps—a step beyond kindergartners and first graders.

Josh: Why Middle School Matters

Josh is eleven years old and in the sixth grade. He's part of the "middle school" trend of recent decades.

Not long ago, sixth grade was the final grade of elementary school. Seventh, eighth, and ninth grades combined to form junior high. By 1993, however, only 13% of the 12,100 total middle level schools were following that "junior high" model (McEwin, et al, 1995). The majority of middle level schools combined the sixth through eighth grades into "middle schools" like the one Josh attends. Most school administrators consider the sixth-through-eighth-grade configuration to be the most appropriate to meet the developmental needs of children (Valentine, et al, 1993).

At eleven, Josh is beginning to assert some independence from his parents. His friends receive far more of his attention and concern than ever before. He's under a lot of pressure to conform to his group of peers (Slavin 1994). He faces some threats—ranging from gangs to drugs—that his parents and teachers never had to face at his age. He's immersed in media and sports. He deeply desires to reach the next stage of his development.

Further, Josh is beginning to understand figurative speech and parables that younger students can't. And he's faced an enormous shift in his weekday school experience—teachers, buildings, and his schedule have all changed (Schickedanz, et al, 1990).

The issues Josh faces have also experienced a significant shift. The middle school years are marked by change at a pace students have never experienced before. The need for a sense of stability suddenly comes to the forefront.

So Josh comes to Sunday school. Under traditional age grouping, he's placed in a Sunday school class with fifth graders he never sees during the week. He feels "put back" because of the age of his classmates and the material they use. After all, *he's not in elementary school anymore.* He acts bored in class. The teacher thinks it must be something wrong with the way she teaches. But in this case, it's another issue: Josh feels left out because he doesn't "fit" in the Sunday school learning environment (Video 1998).

Our suggestion: *Group sixth through eighth graders together,* especially if the schools in your community do the same. (It would follow, then, that you'd group ninth through twelfth grades together into a high school class.) *Group fourth and fifth graders in a class of their own*, where they can begin the transition from Bible stories to Bible studies. The middle school class should be able to handle more complex and abstract concepts as they launch into this type of thinking. One last note: ninth grade Sunday school students will also feel "put back" if they are grouped with middle schoolers instead of high schoolers—especially if their weekday school places them in high school.

What Are They Thinking?

From birth to age two, most of what goes into a child's mind is affected by his or her senses and movement. We call this *sensorimotor thinking*. At this age, kids are stockpiling massive amounts of information, but not really classifying that data.

Around preschool age, kids are able to focus on single aspects of situations. For example, if you pour a certain amount of water from a tall glass into a bowl, they will still believe there was more water in the glass because of the most significant single aspect in their minds—the height of the glass. This type of thought process is known as *single-aspect* or *preoperational thinking*.

Because most toddlers have not taken this step in their thinking, there can be some friction when they are grouped with preschoolers.

Around the second grade, kids are able to understand the relationships between multiple aspects of the same situation. This is known as *logical* or *concrete operational thinking*.

Because most first graders have not made it to this stage in their thinking, they experience some confusion when grouped with second graders.

Around the sixth grade, kids begin to be able to handle abstract concepts like "grace" and "atonement." This type of thought process is called *abstract* or *formal operational thinking*.

Most fifth graders have not taken this step in their thinking; therefore, it is better to group fifth graders with fourth graders, while grouping sixth graders with seventh and eighth graders.

A New Look at Grouping Options

Here's a summary of our revised suggestions for Sunday school age groupings:

<u>Age</u>	<u>Grouping</u>
18 months through two years	*Toddlers & Twos*
Three through five year olds	*Preschool*
Kindergarten and 1st Graders	*Early Elementary*
2nd and 3rd Graders	*Elementary*
4th and 5th Graders	*Upper Elementary*
6th through 8th Graders	*Middle School*
9th through 12th Graders	*High School*

So are more teachers needed to make this work? No! In this developmentally-sensitive grouping, the number of classes remains the same as a traditional grouping. More detailed reasons for these groupings are offered in the age-specific chapters that follow.

Grouping Options for Small Churches

Fewer students and fewer teachers could make it necessary to put a wider range of ages in the same class. The challenge is to meet the needs of all the students in your classes. That means you need to avoid talking over the heads of younger students while not talking down to the older ones.

We recommend the following groupings because the students in each grouping share some significant developmental characteristics. That should help students to work together well—and give teachers that sweet feeling of success.

Group 1: Birth through Two Year Olds—These children don't participate in group activities. They have a short attention span and need nurturing. Even some physical needs must be met, like diapering. These children have limited verbal skills and learn best through exploration; therefore, they need a safe classroom environment for play and roaming.

You need enough adults help to ensure that each child receives individual attention at some time during the class. Tell Bible stories one-on-one with individual children. Repeat stories and songs several times. A curriculum written for toddlers and two year olds is probably your best option.

Group 2: Three to Six Year Olds (PreK–First Grade)—These children love to work with their developing verbal and small muscle skills. Unlike the kids in Group 1, these children enjoy working in groups. They like listening to stories, but remember to offer them a variety of activities. These children are non-readers or beginning readers, so a curriculum written for early elementary students will probably work best.

Set up learning centers for this class. Remember to adapt curriculum activities for younger children in the class as needed. Small muscle skills needed to handle pencils and scissors might still be developing in younger students, so pre-cut projects or team older children with younger ones as "buddies."

Group 3: Seven to Ten Year Olds (Second through Fifth Grades)—These students are beginning to think more logically. They want to share their opinions and knowledge, and, for the most part, are able to read and write independently. They enjoy active games and socializing. They're very concerned with rules and fairness.

Use curriculum that best matches the ages of the majority of your students. Group students with their peers for activities unless a younger student would benefit from the experience of an older student. Older students can help you with some responsibilities like reading portions of the Bible story or organizing activities. These students can learn from listening to each other. Be sure to recognize the contributions of every student by repeating or rewording those contributions—or simply thanking the student and moving on.

Group 4: Middle/High School—These students expect to be treated differently than children. They are strongly influenced by peers and work well in small groups or teams. They can think abstractly, and tend to contemplate ideas before sharing. They respond well to open-ended questions. More than any other age group, they tend to be influenced by what is popular or current.

If you have to combine middle and high schoolers, we recommend using a high school curriculum. You'll want to refer to the combined group by one name, such as "youth" or "teens." Encourage activities outside the class that will help the group bond together. During activities, use your judgment whether to put students with peers or with a classmate who is older or younger. Again, make sure that you recognize every student contribution. (Here, a simple "thanks" or repeating their input will suffice.)

Here's a recap of these grouping options *for small churches*:

Age	_Grouping_
Birth through two year olds	*Toddlers & Twos*
Three to six year olds	*PreK–First Grade*
Seven to ten year olds	*Second–Fifth Grade*
Middle/High Schoolers	*Youth*

Are there any exceptionally difficult classes in your church's Sunday school? How might some of those problems be addressed through more appropriate age groupings?

Whatever the size of your Sunday school, it is to the teachers' and students' advantage to *group classes according to the learning characteristics of your students*.

These learning characteristics are usually indicated by the *age and development* of your students. Traditional Sunday school age grouping "misses" the developmental location of some groups of students. Our suggested revisions for age groupings—and age groupings for smaller churches—take student learning characteristics into account. These revisions should make it easier for your Sunday school instructors to reach *every* one they teach.

Chapter 4

Toddlers & Twos:
How to Teach the
Observant Imitators

Lisa is a cute-as-a-button two year old full of energy and imagination. She goes on her own adventures every day. She reaches the four corners of her world well before any well-marketed television character can interrupt her. Typically two, Lisa is exuberant about any discovery she makes—for about thirty seconds.

So how might anyone captivate a two year old like Lisa? Can anything about God get through to a child that age?

Lisa's minister reports that one Sunday morning following praise and worship the congregation spent a few moments in silent adoration. As they considered God's majesty together a small, clear voice broke through the stillness: "The Lord is a great God . . ." Gently, and insistently, Lisa sang out her thoughts to God while perched atop a front-row pew near the center aisle. As the phrase *repeated, people slowly lifted their eyes, turning to find the source of the song.*

What they saw was a little two-year-old child, eyes shut, singing this simple phrase of God's greatness. The simplicity of Lisa's devotion was stunning. The adult congregation was treated to a renewed awareness of God.

And the minister remembered a familiar verse from Matthew's Gospel: "From the lips of children and infants, you have ordained praise" (Matt. 21:16b).

Toddlers & Twos: The Observant Imitators

Who knows what gets through to a two year old? Lisa had heard this familiar phrase of a praise song again and again. Like most two year olds, she was ready to *imitate* what she heard. She had seen adults sing praise to God in the worship service. She was *experimenting* with her own role of participation in that service.

Lisa demonstrated she was learning the *language* of worship alongside her own developing language skills. And she was learning in the context of important *relationships*. Obviously she felt comfortable enough around the adults in church to follow their pattern. Yet her personal expression of praise—given regardless of the behavior of the rest of the group—shows a *self-contained* point of reference.

Lisa is "totally two." Her brain, like those of other two year olds, is as active as an adult's. It has developed from birth at a staggering rate. From all indications, she's biologically primed for learning (Shore 1997).

One thing that recent research has proven is that you can't teach a two year old like a three year old because their learning patterns are drastically different. (We realize this could have an impact on your present strategy of age-grouping students. If this is the case, take a look at Chapter 3 for some age-grouping options.)

You've seen two year olds pretend they're sleeping. It's hard for them not to smile. They stick their thumbs in their mouths, tilt their heads to one side, and close their eyes. They *copy the ritual they've learned* about sleeping. You've probably watched a two year old take a plastic block and call it "doggie." He'll move it around and make barking and growling sounds. He's *copying the behavior he associates* with a dog.

This type of symbolic play appears for most of us between the ages of eighteen months and just before three years. It's an exciting means of learning for a two year old. One key element of this special learning function is *imitation*. Two year olds are always ready to imitate your movements, language, and expressions if given the opportunity (Piaget & Inhelder 1969).

Sometimes the best way to find out what connects with two year olds is to listen to what they imitate while they're *experimenting*. (Many parents have rightly concluded that their own language has to change once they hear their toddlers imitating them! Hopefully those imitation experiments won't happen in a situation that's *too* embarrassing.)

Children have never been very good at listening to their elders, but they have never failed to imitate them. — James Baldwin

What drives a two year old to experiment? The appreciation of their senses. Two year olds touch, taste, feel, and smell their environment at a rate that would seem like overload to any other age group. That's why it takes them so long to cover even a short distance on their own. They have to make contact with everything along the way (Ames, et al, 1979).

What two year old doesn't love a story? What parent doesn't remember the excitement a toddler has when she attaches words to objects? Toddlers and twos are developing *language* skills. Verbal stimulation helps them develop. Their vocabulary might range from five to 1,000 words, but will seem to grow by leaps and bounds. They love any activity that uses words: conversation, singing, identifying objects, reading stories. Their listening and interest levels are far beyond their ability to respond (Schickedanz, et al, 1990).

Children learn best in the context of important *relationships*. Toddlers and two year olds are no exception. This is a crucial time for teachers to demonstrate the love of Christ.

It is also a crucial time to demonstrate a one-on-one interest in the children. TV or videos cannot replace your presence in a two year old's life. You act as a guide to the child's environment. You take care to talk in ways—like using short sentences—that a two year old can easily understand. You provide the content for the mystery of language (Kotulak 1996).

Two year olds are "*self-contained*." Watch them closely. You may see them playing *next to* each other, but you won't likely see them playing *with* each other. Their pretend play is usually solitary until they reach the age of three (Schickedanz, et al 1990). The group approach to teaching that works so well with older preschoolers will be frustrating if you're teaching two year olds. Any grouping of threes and twos will be brief— and surprisingly impersonal. Cooperation and sharing haven't yet entered their personalities (Ames, et al, 1979).

The Ways Two Year Olds Learn

● ● ● ● ● ● ● ●

Lisa's learning characteristics don't diminish her simple faith in the least. In fact, those characteristics show how two year olds operate.

Two year olds are:

(1) imitators;
(2) experimenters;
(3) learning language skills;
(4) learning through important relationships; and
(5) self-contained.

Working with these characteristics—which define the way two year olds learn— will help you reach these little ones.

Imitation. Experimentation. Language development. Relationships. Self-containment. Each is a key to how a two-year-old learns.

And every one of those keys can be implemented as you teach.

Teaching to Reach Toddlers & Two Year Olds

Because two year olds learn by *imitation,* be sure to offer input that they can copy. Talk in short sentences. Encourage them to repeat stories and actions. Sing simple action songs. Help them learn by doing.

Two year olds *experiment.* Your classroom, then, needs to be a safe environment for exploration and free play. Allow them time to explore, and time to watch. Give them opportunities to use their eyes, hands, ears, noses, and mouths to learn. Do crafts that emphasize the process rather than the product. (And don't forget to allow for personal needs—like potty training—in your classroom environment.)

To encourage their development in *language,* offer stories, songs and discussions at a beginning language level. Encourage them to talk. Repeat their words back to them.

The *relationships* you build with two year olds should demonstrate that you care about them. Any adult working with two year olds needs to be active with them. Take an interest in what's going on with their lives.

Because toddlers and twos are *self-contained,* don't expect them to respond well to large-group activities. Ideally, you need to address them one-on-one. They can handle brief small-group times, but the group should not exceed four to six. Dealing well with this learning characteristic may require more than one adult in your classroom. But the advantage of this age group is that these children—in a contained, safe, and stimulating classroom—can largely occupy themselves in play while you're talking with one of their classmates.

The Natural Learning Cycle* and Toddler/Twos

As a *motivator,* you're providing a *context for learning.* As you teach toddlers and two year olds, you'll need to encourage each child to find an activity as they enter your classroom. Offer a child

See Chapter 2 to learn more about the Natural Learning Cycle.

a specific toy. Join the children in playing: build a block tower or have a pretend tea party with them. You might consider reading a book to the children. By and large, toddlers and twos will love to sit with you. Have at least three options available to give all the children some time and space to explore.

Debbie remembers, too late, that two year olds learn best through imitation.

Your role as *information giver* in the session means you'll be offering something new to your students. To do that effectively, remember that children at this age don't do well in large groups. Limit the number of children you're giving information to at one time to six (four is better). Try to have a picture or object that is both (1) easily identified by the children and (2) specifically tied in with the lesson's content. Encourage the children to point to, handle, identify, and talk about the picture or object. You'll probably want to memorize the content ahead of time (a story is usually best for this age), so you can do actions as you tell it. When telling a Bible story, leave a Bible open and let the children know that your story comes from the Scriptures. That will help them make the connection between your Sunday school sessions and God's Word. Remember to keep your sentences short and your words simple. And plan enough time into your session to repeat this step with the children. Repetition of both words and actions will help the children learn and remember.

As a *coach* of toddlers and two year olds, you'll help the children discover how what they've learned can apply to everyday life. "Coaching" here means engaging the children in activities that let them encounter the key point of the lesson in several different but repetitive ways. Offer the application in the simplest ways you can. Make your coaching time as much of a one-on-one situation as possible. When you've released children from the small group experience, go and visit them where they are in the classroom to coach them. A popular method for toddlers and twos is the use of a mobile felt board—a smaller version of the flannel graphs you may have known in Sunday school. The felt board allows each child the opportunity to manipulate figures and become a "storyteller" themselves. The overall experience again serves to reinforce what the children learn.

As an *encourager*, you'll be helping toddlers and two year olds do something creative to reinforce the lesson. Usually leading the children through some kind of craft works best here. At this age, children need to be encouraged through the *process* of creativity rather than the end *product*. As they draw, for instance, you need to remember that their drawings aren't meant to represent anything. The ability to try to draw specific things doesn't come along until age three (Piaget & Inhelder 1969). So the crafts here need to encourage simple physical involvement—and that needs to be your goal in offering them. Resist the urge to do the craft *for* the children. Instead, let them have fun in the process. If possible, let each child do the craft project more than once and choose the best one to take home.

Toddlers and two year olds learn through *imitation, experimentation, and important relationships*. They are quickly developing *language skills*. They tend to be *self-contained*, and so do better apart from "whole group" classroom activities.

Do

Create a safe, interesting environment where children can freely explore.

Refer frequently to God, Jesus, and the Bible to lay a solid foundation for future spiritual growth.

Present Bible stories in brief, short presentations, encouraging movement and participation by the children.

Encourage lots of talking and repeating.

Teach children individually or in small groups.

Encourage crafts and projects which allow children to enjoy the process of creating.

WHAT WORKS   WHAT DOESN'T

Don't

Don't have any unsafe conditions which would keep the children from securely moving about.

Don't assume that toddlers are too young to be exposed to Bible truths.

Don't tell lengthy Bible stories as children sit passively.

Don't discourage children from talking and interacting.

Don't teach the whole class at one time if the class size is large.

Don't pass out craft activities which require coloring in lines or in which all the crafts look exactly the same when finished.

Curriculum
Check

Does your toddler curriculum require you to work with toddlers in groups, or does it provide opportunities to spend time with the children one-on-one?

✓ Does your toddler curriculum work best when children sit quietly, or is it designed to work with children as they talk and move about freely?

✓ Does your toddler curriculum expect that all crafts will look the same when finished, or does it encourage the creative process?

✓ Does your toddler curriculum assume that the most you can do is babysit and entertain children, or does it encourage meaningful learning about Bible truths at a simple level?

What three things do you feel best about in your class for toddlers and twos? Why? What idea(s) from this chapter can you try to use in your next session?

Chapter 5

Preschoolers (3-5 years): How to Teach the 'Why' Questioners

Not long ago Rosann received a letter from a veteran Sunday school teacher in San Antonio, Texas. It encouraged us greatly about the potential of preschoolers. Here's part of it:

I met Mark for the first time, years ago, when he joined our preschool class. My first impressions of him surrounded his active social life. It wasn't long before he had made friends with every four-year-old girl in my class—that is, when he wasn't kicking their shins under the learning center tables.

However, my lasting impression of Mark surrounds his curiosity. He was on an unending quest for information. Sometimes I became frustrated as Mark questioned seemingly everything that I did or asked of the class. "Why? Why? Why?" became the banner over the preschool class that year. It was contagious. I think Mark infected the whole class with this hunger for meaning. It wasn't long before our class became a year-long journey for unexplored knowledge.

Mark was from a military family. They were in and out of our church in less than a year. But last spring I heard a knock on my front door late one Saturday morning. When I stepped onto the front porch, there was a handsome young man with the most beautiful bouquet of red roses I'd ever seen.

"Are you Mrs. Larsen?" he inquired.

"Yes," I replied, a little amazed. "Who are these flowers for?"

"They're for you, ma'am. I'm Mark Langley. Do you remember me? I was in your Sunday school class when I was four years old."

It was Mark, all right. His curious eyes sparkled just as they had years ago. Mark sat out on the front porch with me and updated his life's story. He had just completed his doctoral thesis in molecular biology. The title was so serious-sounding and technical that I could never pronounce most of it, much less understand it. But I do remember how it began: "Why human cells . . ."

As he showed me the cover page I noticed he had circled the "Why" in red marker. "This part of my thesis belongs to you, Mrs. Larsen. That's why I'm bringing you flowers today. You helped me discover that it's okay to ask questions and to wonder 'why.'"

The flowers from Mark wilted long ago. But they bloom again in my mind every time I hear a curious preschooler asking "Why?"

Preschoolers: The "Why" Questioners

Not every preschooler will grow up to become a molecular biologist. But every one of them has enough *curiosity* in place to become one. Mark's example also demonstrates a child's social development from being a solitary learner at age two to responding to *group learning* at ages three and above.

TAKE 5 *How do you usually respond when children ask questions in the middle of Sunday school class? Do they feel more like interruptions or opportunities? Why?*

Learning centers were a given in Mark's Sunday school class. Preschoolers love learning centers, especially when those centers offer *large muscle* and *sensory learning* activities.

Preschoolers are only able to focus on one aspect of a situation at a time. Logic has nothing to do with how they think. Fantasy is just as real as reality to them. Truth is usually defined by what they see, smell, hear, taste, or touch. Think about a preschooler's God-given curiosity. Combine it with his need to learn through sensory contact. Then you'll begin to understand how exciting—and how much fun—it can be to teach these children whose favorite single question is "Why?"

Preschoolers are primed for an explosion in learning. Educators long suspected that something dramatic was happening in the brains of preschool children because of the surge in learning that usually takes place for them. Not long ago, pediatric neurologist Harry Chugani measured the activity level of brains at all ages from infancy to old age. He traced the brain's energy level to measure its activity level. He discovered that, beginning in the middle of the preschool years through about age ten, the brain

The Ways Preschoolers Learn

Is it any wonder that preschoolers like Mark ask "Why?" so much? Their brains are hungry for input from a variety of sources—and you're one of them! Preschoolers are:

(1) questioners;
(2) able to focus on only one aspect of a situation at a time;
(3) sensory learners;
(4) able to do many more things physically than toddlers & twos;
(5) group learners; and
(6) roaming learners.

Remember these characteristics as you teach to reach three, four and five year olds.

seemed to glow like a nuclear reactor. The activity level was 225 percent higher than that of adult brains. (You may be thinking, "Aha! That's why I'm having trouble keeping up with those kids!")

What was happening that made the child brain so busy? It wasn't a meltdown. This process is simply a time in their development when the brain is *deciding whether to keep or eliminate connections*. The brain eagerly seeks information from the senses to make these decisions. If the connections aren't reinforced through the senses as the brain builds a child's mental architecture, they go away (Kotulak 1996).

As we mentioned previously, the learning patterns of a three year old are dramatically different from those of a two year old. That's why we encourage you—if you haven't already—to group two year olds with toddlers, and "graduate" three year olds to the preschool class. (See Chapter 3 for more information and hints on age grouping.)

The brain's active search for information stimulates preschoolers to get that information any way they can. Their brains also drive them to some kinds of behavior that can drive unsuspecting parents and teachers a little crazy. Mud, paint, wet sand, bright colors, happy sounds, and glue are all delights to preschoolers. It's all part of their drive for *sensory learning*. The *learning centers* you establish for the preschool classroom can provide a smorgasbord for your students' senses. They can also offer preschoolers opportunities to show off the developing motor skills they just didn't have at the age of two. Preschoolers can use markers, crayons, and pencils. Their improving small muscle skills and finger movement allows them to put pegs in a board, string beads, and cut paper, too (Schickedanz, et al, 1990).

Physical changes mark children in their preschool years. Large muscle development allows them to be more physically active. They become longer and leaner. Baby fat and toddler tummies tend to disappear. Their legs lengthen. The combined effect moves their center of gravity to the abdomen. That means they're ready to jump, run, and climb—and roam about your classroom (Schickedanz, et al, 1990).

And then there's the consistent *questioning*: "Why? How come? What's that?" Until you come up with an answer suitable to them— whatever it may be—preschoolers can sound like a broken record with their 'why' questions. But remember: preschoolers *aren't* seeking a comprehensive "big picture" answer as much as one that responds directly and simply to their real question.

One classic example: Danny came to his mother late one morning asking, "Where did I come from?" His mother Leslie swallowed hard. She'd hoped that question would have been put off for several years. Praying Danny would forget the question if she stalled she replied, "We should talk about that later." But Danny, a typical four year old, kept asking "Where did I come from?" with greater intensity and frequency through lunch and into the afternoon. So Leslie began a delicate, thorough explanation of God's miracle of reproduction. Danny responded with a confused look after a minute or so. Leslie asked, "Honey, do you have a question?" Danny said, "Yeah. Where did I come from? Ben said he was from Des Moines. Where did *I* come from?"

Danny was looking for an answer to clarify one aspect of his situation. Preschoolers don't relate to "big picture" answers. They're not ready to follow a complicated process of relationships. That's because they're *single-aspect thinkers*, that is, they are only able to focus on one aspect of a situation at a time.

Logic processes aren't developed in the preschooler. Pour every drop of fingerpaint from a tall container into a short, wide one. A preschooler will firmly believe that the tall container had more fingerpaint. The child can only focus on one aspect of the situation—in this case, the height of the container (Slavin 1994).

Preschoolers *can* learn by themselves, but unlike two year olds, they actually enjoy one another's company. They enjoy the challenges and stimulation other children offer. They often guide the behavior of other children. They have a strong group identification. Therefore, preschoolers are ready for group learning (Ames, et al, 1979). Make-believe or "pretend play" dominates the preschool stage in a child's development. They love transforming themselves into someone or something else. That kind of transformation prepares them to think more abstractly and imaginatively when they get older. Pretend play also enhances a child's cognitive, social, and language development (Slavin 1994).

Using pretend play or dramatization is a great way to review lesson content.

Preschoolers are the "why" questioners. They focus on one aspect of a situation at a time. They appreciate group learning far more than when they were two. They love sensory learning and learning centers, and are physically developed enough to take advantage of them.

Single-aspect thinking makes the preschool age a prime time to focus on the truth. This is the age to convince children, "I love Jesus and Jesus loves me." Rosann remembers a recent experience with a four year old she taught:

Emily looked at me with huge brown eyes and said with great sincerity, "I love Barney [the dinosaur] and Barney loves me." She believed this absolutely. There was no logic involved. This was a fact to her.

The fact that Barney actually did not know she existed never entered her mind. He spoke to her on the TV. That was enough to establish truth to a four year old. It made my role in Emily's life come into focus: I must be the conduit who demonstrates the love of Jesus to her. Jesus is not visually present to convince her He loves her. Jesus isn't on TV. But Emily can see, hear, and touch me— and that's what she and her preschool buddies will grasp and believe to be the whole truth.

I must be the one who keeps showing Emily and her classmates the love of Jesus until it becomes a simple fact for them: "Jesus loves me."

As a Sunday school teacher, you can represent the love of Jesus to a preschooler as few others can. Be God's "conduit." If ever there is an age where this role can work, this is it.

Teaching to Reach Preschoolers

Preschoolers are *questioners.* So as you teach, give them plenty of opportunities for observation and involvement. They're wonderfully curious—and because they're *sensory learners* the more interactive contact you can provide with learning material the better. Encourage your preschoolers in the creative process; don't choose craft projects where the adults do most of the work and the children merely do the assembling or put on the final touches.

Discussions allow preschoolers to use their developing vocabularies; talks like these also give the teacher opportunities to ask "What do you think?" when a child asks "Why?" But remember to keep a preschooler's short attention span in mind as you discuss.

"Okay, Billy, your job is to paint two dots for eyes."

Because preschoolers focus on single aspects of situations, their logic processes aren't developed. Provide opportunities for play and make-believe. Simple roleplaying can be a great review for lesson content.

What do you enjoy best about teaching preschoolers?
What challenges you the most about teaching preschoolers?

Preschoolers are able to do much more than toddlers & twos. Take advantage of their increased muscle and verbal skills, and celebrate their progress with them. They love to show and tell what they can do, so allow for that. Because they're not as self-contained, you can use *group learning* experiences in the classroom. Their short attention spans combined with their need for a variety of activities make them *roaming learners*. Therefore, the use of learning centers is a great strategy for your preschool classroom.

The Natural Learning Cycle* and Preschoolers

As a *motivator*, you'll offer a *context for learning.* You could employ learning centers even before class that help connect the children's lives to the upcoming lesson content. You might decide to begin your class session with a time of talking and interaction. Wait silently for a moment after you ask a question. That will allow children time to think. If there's no response to a question, reword it or offer an example of an answer. Help the children respect each other's answers and contributions, too.

As you offer the lesson content in your role as *information giver*, consider offering the content in the form of a story. Telling the story, as opposed to reading it, is more effective for preschoolers. Use actions, facial expressions, and varied voices to create interest. Songs and rhymes are also great options for presenting lesson content. Make sure that the means you use to present information lends itself to repetition. Whatever you use, encourage your preschoolers to ask their own questions about the lesson.

As a *coach*, you're helping the children discover how they can take what they've learned and apply it to everyday life. Give your preschoolers an environment that encourages them to explore options. Keep your classroom varied with learning centers structured in a variety of ways. Use floor space and table space. Offer several activities for this step. Sometimes you can let the children choose one activity to do for the allotted time. Or, you could have small groups (remember, they're safe at this age) rotate to all the activities. For some children, the independent exploration of this step will be the most beneficial.

The final lesson step puts you in the role of *encourager.* Here, help your preschoolers do something creative to reinforce the lesson. It could be a craft or an activity that encourages them to come up with ideas of their own. (But at this age, you may need to show them some ways to apply those ideas.) A group brainstorming session could produce a wide variety of ideas from which the children make individual choices. Resist the urge to tell the children what they "should" get out of the lesson. Trust God's Spirit to help them recognize just what they need, and to lead them to their own application.

*See Chapter 2 to learn more about the Natural Learning Cycle.

Preschoolers are *questioners*. They focus on single aspects of situations. What they lack in logic skills is more than made up for through their curiosity. They're *sensory learners* who enjoy the variety and stimulation of learning centers. Their *development beyond the toddler/two stage* makes them able to benefit from *group learning* and *roaming* in the classroom.

Do

Tell the Bible story with the Bible open at the appropriate passage to reinforce the fact that the stories come from the Bible and that they are true.

Provide activities that allow children to use their large muscle skills.

Offer choices of activities—varied learning centers with options that use as many of their senses as possible.

Don't

Don't concentrate so much on making the Bible stories entertaining that the children miss the point that the stories come from the Bible, which came from God.

Don't expect preschool children to sit quietly for long periods of time.

Don't have only one activity for all children.

Do

Provide opportunities for children to practice their developing finger dexterity skills such as cutting, coloring, sorting, and stringing.

Have creative play experiences—roleplaying, dramatization, music, and movement.

Allow their expanding vocabularies to be stretched through small group discussions and shared projects.

Encourage their natural curiosity by valuing their questions.

Don't

Don't give children craft activities where the adult has done most of the work and the children merely do the assembly.

Don't expect preschool children to be the audience and not the participants.

Don't be the one to always do all the talking.

Don't discourage or ignore the constant "whys" you will hear.

Curriculum
Check

✓ Does your preschool curriculum play down the fact that your stories come from God's Word, or does it emphasize that your stories come from the Bible, which was given to us by God?

✓ Does your preschool curriculum have crafts that must be done mostly by the teacher, or does it provide ample opportunities for your students to work with their hands?

✓ Does your preschool curriculum have all the children doing the same thing, or does it offer a variety of creative play experiences?

✓ Does your preschool curriculum assume that students will be sitting still most of the class, or does it provide opportunities for students to use their large muscle skills?

✓ Does your preschool curriculum have the teacher do most of the talking, or do children have many opportunities to speak—to the teacher and to each other?

What three things do you feel best about in your preschooler class? Why? What idea(s) from this chapter can you try to use in your next session?

Chapter 6

Early Elementary Children (Kindergarten–First Grade): How to Teach the Creative Dramatists

It's always an encouragement to hear from parents who keep themselves aware of the events in their children's Sunday school classes. Rosann heard from one such parent in Cleveland who helped her child connect what she was learning in Sunday school to a friend in need:

Our youngest daughter, Megan, was devastated by the news. Her best friend and next-door neighbor Jeremy was diagnosed with leukemia. Within three months Jeremy was hospitalized full-time.

"Mommy, isn't there anything that I can do to make Jeremy better?" Megan sobbed in my lap one day.

I asked her softly, "Honey, what does Jeremy miss the most about not being home? Would he like you to take some of your new toys for him to play with?"

Megan responded with a melancholy pain that didn't seem to fit a first-grade perspective on life. "Jeremy doesn't need more toys. He can't even play with the ones he's got now. What he misses the most is coming to our Sunday school class," she said, "and I can't take that to him."

"You might not be able to take the whole class to Jeremy, but you could take the Bible stories."

Megan sat up straight. "How can I do that? I can't even read the stories myself."

"Megan, you don't have to be able to read to understand the stories. You always come home from Sunday school so excited about how Mrs. Schultz can tell those stories in a way that makes you feel like you're right there in the Bible world," I reminded her. "You could learn to tell the same stories to Jeremy in a way that would make him feel like he was in a different world too. Why don't you learn how to be a storyteller for Jeremy, and take your class to him?"

The next Sunday afternoon was Megan's first trip to see Jeremy with the puppets, masks, and other crafts that she had made in her Sunday school class. It became the high point of the week for both Megan and Jeremy. In fact, Megan didn't miss a single Sunday school class that summer. After all, she wasn't going just to learn for herself; now she was going to learn for Jeremy, too.

Megan would tell and retell the Bible stories to Jeremy each week. He slowly began to improve. Megan felt like the storytelling was the most important treatment Jeremy was receiving. She may have been right. After all, if "faith comes by hearing, and hearing by the word of God" (Romans 10:17), then why couldn't the same well-told Bible story bring the results today that it did the first time it was ever told?

Kindergartners and First Graders: The Creative Dramatists

Megan's mother gave her little girl some wonderful advice because it connected beautifully with Megan's development. Early elementary students love to roleplay and *dramatize* as they learn. So Megan responded enthusiastically to retelling the Sunday school stories she'd learned. The opportunity for *interactive creativity* appeals to children of all ages, but this is especially true for early elementary students because their finger skills are honed to a level that allows them to produce crafts that, by and large, meet their expectations. (It is especially encouraging that Megan's Sunday school class seemed to match her developmental stage, too!)

Early elementary children are still at the stage in their thinking where they will focus on only one aspect of a situation at a time. But they are at the "high end" of this stage, and will occasionally use logic to come to conclusions about the world around them.

Learning to read is a key event for early elementary children. They can absorb information far beyond their ability to read, but many cannot handle material that requires strong reading abilities. That's why storytelling and roleplaying are still the primary means of information-giving. But you can still use printed material that uses short, repetitive sentences and picture-text matching to encourage the emerging and beginning readers in their developing skills.

Have you ever encouraged early elementary students to tell a story back to you? What would be the benefits for the child? for you?

Dramatization and roleplaying are favorite means of learning for early elementary children. This kind of pretend play involves transforming oneself or an object into something or someone else. This kind of activity is believed to encourage cognitive, social, and language development. Pretend play can be frequent and complex in kindergartners and first graders. In fact, pretend play peaks in the early elementary years and declines in middle childhood (Slavin 1994).

Interactive creativity is another milestone of the early elementary years. Nowhere else in a child's development will hand activities—coloring, cutting, pasting, painting, and printing—be such a joy to the child. These children love to build with blocks of any size, and to make things of cardboard, paper, wood, clay, and even mud (Ames, et al, 1979).

Again, like their younger counterparts, early elementary students only focus on single aspects of situations. Because they are at the "high end" of this stage of thinking, they occasionally use logic in their reasoning. But by and large, they are only able to focus on one aspect of a situation at a time—and that aspect will be defined by *their perception.*

Mr. Jones was teaching his first graders how to behave in class. It was the first week of school and he was hoping to communicate some important guidelines to smooth the way for the year of learning to come. He began teaching the classroom manners about asking questions. He said, "When I ask a question, I want you to raise your *right* hand, and then I'll call on you." He raised his right hand to demonstrate, then asked, "Can you all raise your right hands, as I am doing?"

Thirty *left* hands went up. When Mr. Jones raised his right hand, his first-graders imitated his action *as they perceived it.* They were unable to see that since he was facing them, his right hand would be to their left (Slavin 1994).

Rosann recalls one early elementary class that showed her their need to be treated as single-aspect thinkers:

I was excited to present the "Flight to Egypt" story to a group of kindergarten children some years ago. I used great dramatic flair while telling the story.

"And then, in the middle of the night, an angel appeared to Joseph and said, 'Rise! Get up! Take Baby Jesus and Mary and FLEE to Egypt! King Herod wants to find Baby Jesus and kill him!' Joseph knew this was a BIG emergency, so he immediately got up and woke up Mary and Baby Jesus. Joseph put them on a donkey, and they hurried out of town to Egypt."

The room was fairly quiet. I assumed that was because they were enjoying this adventurous story. Then one of the children raised his hand and said, "You're kidding, right?"

The Ways Early Elementary Students Learn

● ● ● ● ● ● ● ●

What a thrilling time in a child's life! You can be a wonderful encouragement to early elementary students. Remember, these children are:

(1) dramatists and role-players;

(2) hands-on creators;

(3) at the "high end" of single-aspect thinking; and

(4) almost consumed by the process of learning to read.

Keep these characteristics in mind as you teach to reach your early elementary students.

I was taken aback. I replied, "No, the Bible is true. This is a true story."

"But I thought you said this was an emergency."

I explained the great danger that Jesus, Joseph, and Mary were in—and that it WAS a great emergency.

"Well," the kindergartner continued, "what if King Herod had a Harley? Do you know how fast he could catch up with a DONKEY?"

One charming little girl tried to help me out. "What the teacher meant was, they took the donkey to the AIRPORT."

Soon I lost complete control. Comments started to fly like, "I can walk faster than a donkey!" "Joseph was pretty dumb." In a matter of minutes, I'd lost them. Instead of recognizing that Joseph had been entrusted with an awesome responsibility, they all decided that Joseph had the IQ of coleslaw.

I learned to treat early elementary students like the single-aspect thinkers they are. I should have realized that all new information they process is connected to what they already know. If I had taken a few minutes to discuss travel today versus travel long ago, the children would have been better equipped to understand the content of the Bible story. *(For example, I could have said, "Now we use cars and jets and vans to travel. Then there were no cars or planes. People used animals to take long trips.")*

The primary educational event for early elementary children is *learning to read*. The development of writing skills goes along with reading. These

Charlene knew the children enjoyed her dramatic readings of Bible stories, but she had no idea they were scoring her performance.

children enjoy the challenges of printing. Most of them can print their numbers from 1 to 11 at age six. Girls have mastered their first and last names by age six; boys, by age six-and-a-half. But the letters and numbers tend to be large, labored, uneven, and often reversed (Ames, et al, 1979).

Early elementary children who have been exposed to many books in read-aloud experiences may have made a connection between the written symbols in a book and the stories they've heard—even before they entered school. But children without such experiences may need to encounter a great number of books in school to understand simple conventions about print—for example, you read books from left to right, or that printed symbols have meaning (Englebretson, et al, 1997). So even though the world of reading is being opened to these students, they need to be given adequate and age-appropriate experiences to launch into that world.

Chapter 3 gave our reasons for grouping kindergartners with first graders. First graders and kindergartners are still single-aspect thinkers. By the time a child reaches second grade, she has almost certainly crossed the line into logical thinking. Pretend play won't be as important, then, to the second grader—while to the first grader is it still an important means of processing information. Also, remember that it's far more difficult to create material that covers the huge reading disparity between first and second graders than it is to create material that is comfortable for both kindergartners and first graders.

The age of six seems to be a critical "crossing-over" point for children. By age six, children have mastered most motor skills. They can use their physical skills to achieve goals. They start to understand classes or categories of objects and the relationships between them. They're ready to absorb an enormous amount of information about their social and physical worlds. They use almost completely mature speech as they express their ideas, wants, needs, and experiences. They're learning more rules about appropriate behavior and rules. They're becoming more socially adept (Slavin 1994).

A child is apt to see certain things better than his elders, I think, because, less sure than they of what to expect, he is more apt than they to see what, actually though unexpectedly, is. — Frederick Buechner

Teaching to Reach Early Elementary Children

Early elementary students are *dramatists.* Roleplaying reaches its peak at this stage of a child's development. That means they'll respond to stories—and they'll tell stories they've made up or learned. In fact, asking early elementary students to retell stories is a great strategy for evaluating comprehension. Retelling can even be an alternative to teacher follow-up questions. Allow your students to tell in their own words what they have understood. Keep the setting informal and relaxed. Retelling will help the language and reading comprehension skills of your students, too (Routman 1991).

Early elementary students' love for drama and roleplaying can easily be tied into their aptitude for *interactive creativity*. They can create their own puppets and puppet shows, for example, to retell the lesson content. Their craft projects can illustrate a lesson point. They can come up with unique actions to go along with music.

Single-aspect thinking still dominates early elementary students. Remember to tie in any new learning with their present experience. Don't expect them to recognize complex relationships or ideas. Keep the lesson content focused and simple.

Because early elementary students are *learning to read*, classroom material needs to match their reading abilities. Material that demands too much reading ability is doomed to fail. Short, repetitive sentences with picture-text matching is the best reading material for these students. Curriculum should challenge their thinking and give them opportunities to provide verbal evidence that they've learned the material. And remember, retelling will complement their developing reading skills.

What do you enjoy best about teaching early elementary students? What challenges you the most about teaching them?

The Natural Learning Cycle* and Early Elementary Children

Early elementary children need a *context for learning*. As you follow the Natural Learning Cycle, you'll provide that context in your role as a *motivator*. You might decide to begin your class session with an activity to focus children's attention, followed by a time of talking and interaction. You could allow several seconds of silent "think time" after you ask a question to give the children some time to gather their thoughts. If the children still hesitate to answer, reword the question. You could even give an example of an answer. Be sure to somehow acknowledge each child's answer, whether you simply thank the child or reword her answer.

See Chapter 2 to learn more about the Natural Learning Cycle.

Here's another helpful hint that works well as you help early elementary children discuss: Designate a "talking object" like a pencil or a small ball. During discussion time, a child may talk only if it is his turn to hold the "talking object." Otherwise, it's his job to listen.

Storytelling is still the most powerful way to offer lesson content in your role as *information giver.* Rehearsing a Bible story is an important step in effective delivery. It will be easier to keep your students' attention if you maintain eye contact with them during the story. Practice with any teaching aids or props. Learn the story well enough so you can retell it without reading it. Adjust your facial expressions, vocal tone, volume, pace, and expression as you tell the story. Remember to show the children where the story is found in the Bible. Early elementary students can also handle simple memorization. Be sure to help them understand how the verse connects to the lesson.

Step 3 of the Learning Cycle puts you in the role of *coach* as you help your students understand how the lesson content "works." As with preschoolers, learning centers can be used effectively with early elementary students. Structure the classroom to help them to explore options. Offer several activities for this step. Sometimes you can let the children choose one activity to do for the allotted time. Or, you could have small groups rotate to all the activities. You could also set behavior expectations and then let them explore on their own. At this age, you can trust the children to seek the best activity for them.

In your role of *encourager* in the final Learning Cycle step, your task is to help the children connect the lesson to their lives. You need to both reinforce what they have learned and encourage them to come up with ways they can use their new knowledge. A group brainstorming session could be a good tactic that helps children come up with ideas of their own. They also need a plan, workable for their age, to help them follow through on their ideas. Resist the urge to tell the children what they "should" get out of the lesson. Trust God's Spirit to help them recognize just what they need, and to lead them to their own application.

Early elementary students are *dramatists*; they love stories and roleplaying as means of learning. They thrive on *interactive creativity* that allows them to cut, paste, paint, mold clay, and make up their own stories. They're on the "high end" of *single-aspect thinking*, which means they'll occasionally use logic—but basically can only focus on one element of a situation. The consuming task for early elementary students is *learning to read*, so material with short, repetitive sentences and picture-text matching works best with them.

Do

Establish eye contact with the children and smile.

Provide reading material that is a match for their reading abilities

Encourage students to show they know exactly what the Bible story is about by retelling the Bible content using dramatization, puppets, or roleplaying.

Don't

Don't underestimate what children will pick up from your facial expressions.

Don't expect most of the children to be able to read complex material.

Don't assume children have understood the Bible content simply because the story is finished.

Do

Promote interactive creativity by providing activity choices which include cutting, constructing, and creating.

Encourage activities that match the learning of new readers—recognizing letters, frequent writing opportunities, repetitive text to read.

Recognize that the most important book these children will ever be exposed to is the Bible.

Don't

Don't pass out worksheets which require no interaction, activity, or response.

Don't ignore the fact that learning to read is a consuming part of their lives.

Don't miss opportunities to relate their new reading abilities to a future of reading the Bible.

Curriculum Check

Does your early elementary curriculum require the children to have advanced reading skills, or can prereaders and beginning readers also feel successful?

✓ Does your early elementary curriculum overemphasize worksheet activities, or do learning activities involve interaction, activity, and response?

Curriculum
Check

✓ Does your early elementary curriculum have all the children doing the same thing, or does it offer a variety of creative learning experiences?

✓ Does your early elementary curriculum encourage reading and storytelling for their own sake, or does it help students anticipate the time when they will be able to read the Bible for themselves?

What three things do you feel best about in your early elementary class? Why? What idea(s) from this chapter can you try to use in your next session?

Chapter 7

Elementary Children (Second and Third Grade): How to Teach the Reality Testers

A justifiably proud grandfather recently reported this event in the lives of two of his granddaughters:

Six-year-old Emily was determined to find out the truth. A Tooth Fairy?—it just wasn't possible. She was determined to expose this fraud.

No one knew that Emily had a tooth come out that very day. She didn't tell Mom. She didn't tell Dad. Her plan was to secretly place the tooth under her pillow and see what happened. No cash, no Tooth Fairy.

That night Emily confided her plan to her big sister, third grader Alli. No one else knew that the tooth was under the pillow. The next morning Emily ran excitedly into the kitchen. Her hand clutched two shiny quarters.

"Mom! Dad! Look at what the Tooth Fairy left for me! I didn't think there would be anything, but look!" Emily raced off to put the money away.

The stunned parents shot each other questioning looks.

"Did you put that there? I didn't do it."

"What in the world happened?"

Alli leaned close to her mother's ear. "Mommy, I know." With all the wisdom of an elementary child, Alli confessed that she took the two quarters from her own bank and slid it under her sister's pillow during the night. Then Alli carefully opened her hand and dropped the small pearly tooth into her mother's lap.

"Alli, why did you do it?"

"You know, Mom, I just couldn't let Emily be disappointed." Alli's mom felt tears welling in her eyes. Long after the Tooth Fairy would assume its proper place as a friendly myth in her children's lives, the generosity and love of Jesus in the heart of Alli would remain a cherished reality.

Second and Third Graders: The Reality Testers

Emily was still questioning the existence of the Tooth Fairy. For Alli, the question was settled. The difference between a six year old and an eight year old might only be two years, but those two years represent significant developmental changes. As illustrated by the story above, seven and eight year olds are starting to use logic to figure out how things work. They're figuring out that many early childhood imaginary characters probably don't exist. Imaginary characters have lost their charm.

Because they've just moved into this phase of thinking, second and third graders love *facts*. The *Guinness Book of World Records*, batting averages, and almanacs become favorites in this stage of development.

The urge to collect things usually happens at this stage of childhood. That's because elementary children thoroughly enjoy exercising their *logic and sorting* abilities. Don't be surprised, then, when your second and third graders start talking about their football card, coin, insect, stamp, or rock collections.

Elementary children operate in clearly-defined terms of "right and wrong." They respond to rules and fairness. They are also beginning to take a person's intention into account as they make moral judgments.

Second and third graders can also work together to accomplish *common group goals.* They demonstrate a greater awareness of—and sensitivity to—what others think and feel. They use those observations to make their way into more complex social interactions. (Alli's response to Emily's situation in the story that opens this chapter is a wonderful example of this growing awareness of others.)

Logical thinking (also called *concrete operational thinking*) emerges in children around the age of seven. In this stage of development, children begin using reason and mental operations to understand situations and think about how things work. These children can approach problems from several different angles—they are no longer limited to focusing on one aspect of a problem as before.

An early elementary child can easily identify two identical lumps of clay as similar. If you take one of those lumps and roll it into a long snake shape as the child looks on, he will tend to focus on the single aspect of shape. He will strongly deny that the two lumps still represent the same amount of clay. But *the elementary student* brings the ability to think about more than one aspect of the situation, and so will understand that the same amount of clay can appear in more than one shape.

Second and third graders can apply concrete operations to situations that directly confront them, or to situations with which they are intimately familiar. They still lack the maturity to think in abstract terms. Still, these children show dramatic gains in their thinking and reasoning abilities (Schickedanz, et al, 1990).

The advent of logical thinking produces a focus on *facts* in second and third graders. This means imaginary characters lose their appeal at this age. The Easter Bunny, Santa Claus, and the Tooth Fairy will likely fall victim to logic during these years. They are in the process of becoming "rational." They develop a hunger for information to feed this completely new way of thinking—and thus the attraction to facts (Schickedanz, et al, 1990).

Logical thinking also drives elementary students to put their *logic and sorting abilities* into action. The brain is simply able to organize information better.

For example, suppose you have ten markers that are so slightly different in length that they must be compared side by side to notice the difference. When asked to put them in order of length, a younger child will keep rearranging the markers until he finally recognizes he has it right. A seven or eight year old will find the smallest of the group, then the next smallest, and so on until the markers are arranged. This child uses a "system"—in this case, always looking for the smallest in the remaining group (Piaget & Inhelder 1969).

An emerging sense of "right and wrong justice" is part of the elementary student's makeup. As social sensitivity develops, so does the recognition that actions have consequences.

Which of these characteristics do you notice most in your class of elementary students?

Personal intention is included along with the results of action in making moral judgments. Jean Piaget once presented children with a pair of stories and asked them which child was more "naughty." In the first story a little boy named John is in his room when he is called to dinner. John went to the dining room right away. But he didn't know that behind the door there was a chair, and on the chair there was a tray with twelve cups on it. As John entered the dining room, the door knocked against the tray—and all 12 cups fell and were broken!

The second story featured Henry, who waited until his mom was out one day to try to get some jam out of the cupboard—which his mom had forbidden. Henry climbed up on a chair and stretched out his arm. But the jam was too high up in the cupboard. As Henry was reaching for it, he knocked over a cup—which fell and broke.

The Ways Elementary Children Learn

● ● ● ● ● ● ●

Elementary students show a clear difference from early elementary children. The second and third graders discussed in this chapter tend to share the following characteristics:

(1) logical thinking;
(2) a love for facts;
(3) demonstrated reasoning and sorting skills;
(4) a sense of "right and wrong" justice; and
(5) cooperation with common group goals.

Your efforts to teach to reach second and third graders should be easier as you keep these attributes in mind.

Most adults wouldn't blame John for breaking 12 cups. John was being obedient as he came to dinner, and he had no idea the 12 cups were behind the door. In contrast, Henry was doing something he wasn't supposed to be doing. He may have only broken one cup, but his intentions weren't very good.

Piaget found that children *under six years of age* judged John (who broke twelve cups) to be "naughtier" than Henry (who only broke one cup) because John broke more cups. They were basing their judgment on the amount of damage done rather than the boys' intentions. *By ages seven and eight*, however, children began to take intention into account and based their judgments according to those intentions. The seven- and eight-year-old children thought Henry was "naughtier" (cited in Schickedanz, et al, 1990).

Elementary students are more socialized than younger children. Their play demonstrates this new sense of cooperation. Their games show a common observance of rules, which are known to all the players. They watch one another to make sure the rules are observed. They exhibit a common spirit of honest competition according to the rules. They accept that some win and others lose. They respect rules, but unlike younger children, will change them if there is a consensus for change (Piaget & Inhelder 1969).

Don't expect sophisticated humor from your elementary students. They can milk a corny joke for days—and find it just as funny as the first

"Orange you glad I didn't say banana?"

Jana had heard her share of corny jokes and puns in her elementary class.

time they said it. Puns also tickle their funny bones, so expect to hear a few groaners (probably the same ones more than once).

The transition into logical thinking that occurs for many children around the second grade drives our suggestion *that second graders be grouped with third graders*—rather than with first graders. Logical thinking completely changes how children deal with fantasy and roleplaying. Group rules are treated differently. Their understanding of justice changes. Just as important, how children process printed material changes dramatically between first and second grade. (See Chapter 3 for more information on age groupings.)

Teaching to Reach Elementary Children

Elementary students are *logical thinkers*. They're learning to separate fantasy from reality. They can understand that the Bible is history, not fiction. They can separate Jesus Christ from the fictional characters of childhood. Their growing ability to reason allows them to make applications from Bible learning. They can develop a few different outcomes from one set of circumstances. Encourage them to use their developing abilities and to share what they're thinking.

Second and third graders are experimenting with logic and reasoning. They love *facts*, even trivia, to feed the process. Their fact-based orientation tends to make them more straightforward. They'll say what they think and they'll ask what they want. You can respond to this characteristic by talking to them factually and straightforwardly.

MENTAL FLEX John Burroughs once wrote, "To treat your facts with imagination is one thing, but to imagine your facts is another." As imaginary figures fall under scrutiny in second and third grades, it is an ideal time to differentiate Jesus Christ as a historical figure for the children you teach— and the Bible as a great source of facts for life!

Their *logic and sorting skills* are an indication that elementary students can understand and apply categories. That means they can learn the basic construction of the Bible (sections, books). They can also use references for Bible verses (book, chapter, verse). Fairness is a key issue to second and third graders due to their strong sense of "right and wrong" justice. They see things in clearly-defined terms. They have strong opinions and a need to be "right." That makes it all the more important for you to listen to them, and to set up a classroom atmosphere where they know everyone's ideas will be respected. In their quest for justice, they will sometimes feel irrational guilt. You can help them reason their way through at least some of those feelings. You might let your second and third graders help you decide on class rules and consequences, and on ways to positively motivate each other to stick with them.

Elementary students respond to *common group goals.* Social structures and rules matter more to them than ever before, and they want to show they have a place in the group. They enjoy having friends, and will develop a group of steady companions. Boys will tend to group with boys and girls with girls. You can successfully structure your class session for both large and small group activities in response to this characteristic, although they will still appreciate some time to pursue individual activity.

What do you enjoy best about teaching elementary students? What challenges you the most about teaching them?

The Natural Learning Cycle* and Early Elementary Children

Your role as *motivator* means you'll offer a *context for learning* to your elementary students. Talking and interaction work well to help second and third graders bring their life experiences from the week into the class. As with any "talk time" with children, allow several seconds of silent "think time" after you ask a question to give the children some time to gather their thoughts. If the children still hesitate to answer, reword the question. You could even give an example of an answer. Be sure to acknowledge each child's answer somehow, whether you simply thank the child or reword her answer. Allow enough time for discussion so that each child—even the quieter ones—has a chance to participate.

The fact that second and third graders are readers modifies your role as *information giver.* In classes with younger children, you'll be more of a storyteller. With second and third graders, you can encourage them to take part in the information giving by letting them read. Be sensitive to young readers who still feel insecure in their skills. You can offer them titles or short reading parts, while assigning longer portions to more experienced readers. If you still have nonreaders in your group, involve them by letting them act out

See Chapter 2 to learn more about the Natural Learning Cycle.

nonreading roles in skits or in acting out roles as others read.
Let children ask and answer their own questions about the story.

You're a *coach* in Step 3 of the Learning Cycle. Here, you'll help your students understand how the lesson content applies to everyday life. Again, learning centers could be used effectively. Structure the classroom for independent exploration. Use table and floor space to "divide" the room—a circle of chairs, a throw rug, a portable chalkboard, even masking tape that sections off a table can designate different learning stations. Offer several activities for this step. Sometimes you can let the children choose one activity to do for the allotted time. Or, you could have small groups rotate to all the activities. Establish expectations for their behavior and then let them explore on their own.

In your role of *encourager* in the final Learning Cycle step, you need to help the children connect the lesson to their lives. You need to both reinforce what they have learned and encourage them to come up with ways they can use their new knowledge. Some children might create a written response, others an interactive task or visual creation as they think creatively about their individual response. As with younger ages, a group brainstorming session could be a good tactic that helps children come up with ideas of their own. Resist the urge to tell the children what they "should" get out of the lesson. Trust God's Spirit to help them recognize just what they need, and to lead them to their own application.

Elementary students are *logical thinkers* who are learning to reason. They are focused on *facts*, often having set aside imaginary characters. Their *logic* and *sorting skills* show that they can understand and apply categories. They operate with a sense of *"right and wrong" justice* that shows itself through strong opinions and a need to be "right." Their social development has brought them to a place where they enjoy pursuing *common group goals*.

Do

Work hard to catch every child being good and make a big deal of it.

Have opportunities for group projects, activities, and interaction.

Provide as much factual and background information as you can when presenting the Bible story.

Encourage students to use their Bibles to find verses and references.

Allow students to make choices between activities.

Enjoy the corny jokes and puns of elementary students.

Don't

Don't simply discipline bad or annoying behavior.

Don't require the children to sit quietly and do all work individually throughout the class.

Don't present Bible stories without giving some sort of context for the stories.

Don't tell students about the Bible content without allowing them the chance to look up verses themselves.

Don't have students do the same thing throughout the lesson.

Don't expect sophisticated humor or adult thinking.

WHAT WORKS   WHAT DOESN'T

Do

Allow students to help create classroom rules.

Don't

Don't underestimate the keen sense of justice the students possess—their rules and enforcement will be much more intense than anything you'd create on your own.

Help students appreciate the fact that God gave us the Bible in order to tell us things about Himself and about us that we wouldn't know otherwise.

Don't present the Bible story as just a good tale.

Curriculum Check

Does your elementary curriculum dictate social-control rules that are imposed on students without their feedback, or does it encourage your students to create classroom and game rules?

✓ **Does your elementary curriculum have every student doing the same thing at the same time, or does it offer a variety of activities for the children?**

Curriculum
Check

✓ Does your elementary curriculum have students passively listening to a Bible story, or does it encourage them to use their Bibles to get more in-depth information?

✓ Does your elementary curriculum present the Bible story as simply a good story, or does it emphasize the story's significance and its divine origin?

What three things do you feel best about in your elementary class? Why? What idea(s) from this chapter can you try to use in your next session?

Chapter 8

Upper Elementary Children (Fourth and Fifth Grade): How to Teach the Members-Only Huddlers

A mother of a fifth-grader in Portland, Oregon, shares this story that illustrates the difference in group dynamics between younger children and upper elementary students:

In her ten years I don't think I had ever seen Carey look this upset. She stormed through the house in tears and ran immediately toward her bedroom. I could see her clenching something tightly in her fist as I followed her.

"Carey," I said softly from her doorway. She turned and ran into my arms.

"Mommy, why do people have to be so mean?"

I silently hugged my little blond fifth grader. After several minutes I asked, "Carey, do you want to tell me what happened today?"

We sat down on her bed as she told her story. Carey had saved up almost two weeks' allowance to buy a special necklace for Abbey, her best friend at school. My husband Todd and I had prayed with Carey for Abbey for some weeks. We'd all noticed Abbey's behavior swing back and forth due to her response to peer pressure coming from a new clique she'd joined. The group was headed by a boy named Evan. The group's influence on the fifth-grade class seemed less than desirable to us.

Abbey had been genuinely happy when Carey had privately given her the friendship necklace that noon in the cafeteria. She couldn't thank Carey enough. So Carey was surprised when Abbey and the little "group" approached her at the bus stop at the end of the school day.

"I have a gift for you, too, Carey," Abbey said with a smirk while Evan and the others watched. "Put out your hand."

Some of the group broke into malicious grins as Carey extended her hand. Abbey dropped the friendship necklace into Carey's open palm. Carey looked down. The necklace had been cut into several pieces. She ran onto the bus and burst into tears.

"Why are people so mean?" she asked again. I didn't have an answer.

The necklace incident opened Carey's eyes to the effects of peer pressure. She began to understand Abbey's motive for ruining the necklace. That helped her understand Abbey's insecurities. Apparently Abbey wasn't too comfortable with the incident either. She soon broke free from Evan's group. A few weeks later Abbey approached Carey. This time she was alone.

"I have a gift for you, Carey. A real gift. Please don't be afraid to take it."

Abbey handed Carey a nicely wrapped package. Carey opened it carefully. Inside was a beautiful sterling necklace.

*"I'm so sorry I wrecked the necklace you gave me, Carey.
I want to be friends again. Please?"*

*The girls hugged. I can't say Carey has forgotten the pain she
went through with Abbey and Evan's group, but she seems to be
wiser. And more forgiving than I could have dreamed.*

Upper Elementary Children: The Members-Only Huddlers

Many of the *learning* characteristics of upper elementary children
are the same as second and third graders. For the sake of those readers who haven't read the previous chapter, we'll repeat those
characteristics in this chapter. But we'll also point out that in fourth
and fifth graders those characteristics have matured.

Social differences distinguish fourth and fifth graders from
younger students. They're marked by the need for *membership*
with a group of peers. Peer relationships matter as never before.
Therefore, response to peer pressure is an emerging issue, as
Abbey's response to Carey in the story above shows. Membership
can also be indicated by what's current and popular. This is the age
where "cool" friends, brand names, and popular activities can define
group language and boundaries.

Their accumulated knowledge gives fourth and fifth graders a
much better basis for critique than their younger counterparts. They
can *analyze* situations. They'll recognize errors in print and inconsistencies in behavior.

As with younger elementary students, fourth and fifth graders
are solidly into *logical thinking*. They use logic to figure out how
things work. They've firmly retired many early childhood imaginary
characters. They're still "concrete" thinkers, however, so classroom
instruction needs to be related to their everyday experience as much
as possible.

Fourth and fifth graders still love *facts*. The *Guinness Book of
World Records*, batting averages, and almanacs remain favorites in
this stage of development. Collections of some kind are usually
flourishing by later elementary years; these students still enjoy
exercising their *logic and sorting* abilities.

Fourth and fifth graders' abilities to *analyze* have developed significantly from their earlier years. Key to these abilities are the students' background knowledge and experience. They can better determine truth—as well as inconsistencies—in the texts they read. This developed skill is also

"So am I unique just like everyone else?"

applied to the analysis of intention. In one study, kindergartners, second graders and fourth graders were shown videotaped scenes of a child destroying an object. The scenes demonstrated intentions ranging from hostile to accidental to "innocent bystander." Researchers clearly showed that the younger the children were, the more difficulty they had in identifying and discriminating intentions (Schickedanz, et al, 1990).

Logical thinking emerges in children around the age of seven. In this stage of development, children use logic and mental operations to understand situations and think about how things work. These children can approach problems from several different aspects—they are no longer limited to a focus on one aspect of a problem as they were before.

The difference between a more developed logical thinker—for example, a ten year old—and a single-aspect thinker at age six shows when the two children are faced with a hypothetical situation. For example, when a ten year old hears, "All purple snakes have four legs. I am hiding a purple snake. How many legs does it have?" he is likely to argue about the existence of a purple snake or a snake having four legs. (The six year old will tell you four legs and want to see the purple snake immediately.) Such reptiles are not found in the "concrete" world. Reasoning about them is problematic, especially for a logical thinker (Kegan 1982).

Upper elementary students can readily apply logical thinking to situations that directly confront them, or to situations with which they are familiar. They still lack the maturity to think in abstract terms, despite continuing gains in their thinking and reasoning abilities (Schickedanz, et al, 1990).

Logical thinking continues to produce a focus on *facts* in upper elementary students. The Easter Bunny, Santa Claus, and the Tooth Fairy have fallen by the wayside in exchange for more developed rational thinking. They still seek information to feed their logical thinking—and thus the attraction to facts (as opposed to purple four-legged snakes) (Schickedanz, et al, 1990).

Logical thinking also drives elementary students to put their *reasoning and sorting abilities* into action. The brain is simply able to organize information better.

The upper elementary years mark what might be considered "the last hurrah" of brain connections. Half of a child's brain connections—or synapses—disappear by puberty due to lack of interaction with the outside world (Kotulak, 1996). This makes the upper elementary age level a critical time to encourage strong brain connections on all aspects of faith and Bible learning.

This is demonstrated through the heavier reading assignments that begin at the upper elementary level. Fourth and fifth graders need to distinguish what is important and focus on it. They need to organize material in such a way as to remember it. To learn efficiently and successfully (in weekday school or Sunday school) students need to be aware of what they know, what is important to know, and how to sort through and master material. At this level, children are able to ask for further explanations or information that clarifies a passage that is unclear to them (Schickedanz, et al, 1990).

"Right and wrong justice" is part of the elementary student's makeup. Upper elementary students are no exception here. The recognition that actions have consequences has developed. But the rules by which justice is determined can change according to the group. Children before the age of seven tend to see rules as originating from an unquestioned authority like parents, government, or God—and, therefore, untouchable. In contrast, upper elementary children regard rules as the result of agreement among contemporaries. They will allow rules to be made or changed by group consensus. Their sense of justice can prevail over obedience—and it can certainly prevail over existing rules if they feel justice has been violated (Piaget & Inhelder 1969).

Upper elementary students continue in cooperative relationships and *common group goals*. As with second and third graders, their play demonstrates this new cooperation. They demonstrate an ever-greater sensitivity to what others think and feel because of their need for membership. They use those observations to make their way into more complex social interactions. Their games show a common observance of rules, which are known to all the players. They watch one another to make sure the rules are observed. They exhibit a common spirit of honest competition according to the rules. They accept that, according to those rules, some win and others lose. Although cooperative groups work well with upper elementary students, fourth and fifth graders also are ready for independent and quiet activities (Piaget and Inhelder 1969).

"Right and wrong justice" still prevails for upper elementary students. They respond to rules and fairness. In fact, somewhere in these years justice can overtake obedience as a normative value. As noted before, these students are able to take intention into account as they make moral judgments.

Membership promotes feelings of self-worth for both boys and girls in the upper elementary grades. Not being accepted can bring serious emotional problems (Slavin 1994). Peer associations can as easily leave out a friend as celebrate the formation of a group. The September 18, 1954, issue of the *New Yorker* published these clubhouse rules of a group of ten-year-old girls that are as true to form today as they were then:

> Do not hit anyone, except Ronny.
>
> Do not use words worse than "brat."
>
> Do not make faces, except at Ronny.
>
> Do not make a hog or pig of yourself.
>
> Do not tattle, except on Ronny.
>
> Do not tell a white lie unless necessary.
>
> Do not steal, except from Ronny.
>
> Do not be a sneak.
>
> Do not destroy other people's property except Ronny's.
>
> Do not be grumpy, except at Ronny.

If you remember your upper elementary years, chances are the rules above made you chuckle. Unless, or course, you were the "Ronny" for your peers (Kegan 1982).

Our suggestion to group fourth and fifth graders together stems from their social development and their learning skills. The "membership" dynamic that defines upper elementary children can be very difficult for a younger child to understand. Yet their form of rebellion is not as blatant as a middle schooler's. Upper elementary students have better analytic skills than younger children, but are not yet able to abstract to the degree that many middle schoolers can. Therefore, this group seems to define itself apart from other ages. (See Chapter 3 for more information about age grouping.)

Which of the above characteristics do you notice most in your class of upper elementary students?

Teaching to Reach Upper Elementary Children

Membership in a group matters deeply to upper elementary children. Cooperative group activities can help provide them with a sense of belonging. You should take care to encourage a classroom atmosphere that includes and accepts every child as important to the group.

Fourth and fifth graders can handle a greater depth of *analysis*. This ability comes from accumulated knowledge. The students who have been "regulars" in your Sunday school classes from early childhood should easily make the transition from the teacher telling stories to guided reading and studying the Bible for themselves. They're ready to ask questions to clarify content if needed.

Upper elementary students are still *logical thinkers*. They've learned how to separate fantasy from reality. They can understand that the Bible is history, not fiction. Their growing ability to reason allows them to make applications from Bible learning. This being said, upper elementary students have yet to

The Ways Upper Elementary Students Learn

These learning characteristics describe your upper elementary students:

(1) an emphasis on group membership;

(2) better analysis of facts and intentions;

(3) logical thinking;

(4) a love for facts;

(5) demonstrated logic and sorting skills;

(6) a strong sense of "right and wrong" justice; and

(7) cooperation with common group goals.

Try to keep these characteristics in mind as you teach to reach your upper elementary students.

become abstract thinkers. Therefore, keep classroom instruction as concrete and experiential as possible (Slavin 1994). For example, "Roman centurion" will be meaningless until it is related to a soldier. The concept of "witnessing" will have no meaning until the children have experienced it or a roleplay of the process of sharing the good news of Jesus with another person.

As with second and third graders, upper elementary students are experimenting with logic and reasoning. They have developed skills for dealing with "whys" and "hows." They still love *facts* that feed those skills. Their fact-based orientation tends to make them straightforward. They'll say what they think and they'll ask what they want. You can respond to this characteristic by talking to them factually and straightforwardly.

Upper elementary students are usually accomplished at understanding and applying categories. They continue in exercising their *logic and sorting skills.* That means they can learn the basic construction of the Bible (sections, books). They can also use references for Bible verses (book, chapter, verse). As they read, they will seek to determine what material is essential and what is not. Encourage them in this process through letting them talk about their ideas.

"Right and wrong" justice drives upper elementary children to see things in clearly defined terms. They have strong opinions and a need to be "right." That makes it all the more important for you to listen to them, and to set up a classroom atmosphere where they know everyone's ideas will be respected. You might let your upper elementary students help you decide on class rules and consequences, and on ways to positively motivate each other to stick with the rules they have created together.

Fourth and fifth graders respond to *common group goals.* Social structures and rules matter more to them than ever before, and they want to show they have a place in the group. They enjoy having friends and will develop a group of steady friends. They'll tend to group boys with boys and girls with girls. You can successfully structure your class session for both large and small group activities in response to this characteristic, although they will still appreciate some time to pursue individual activity.

What do you enjoy best about teaching upper elementary students? What challenges you the most about teaching them?

The Natural Learning Cycle* and Early Elementary Children

Your role as *motivator* means you'll offer a *context for learning* to your elementary students. Talking and interaction work well to help your students bring their life experiences from the week into the class. As with any "talk time" with children, allow several seconds of silent "think time" after you ask a question to give the children some time to gather their thoughts. If the children still hesitate to answer, reword the question yourself or ask a student to reword it. You might allow the students to work in pairs so they can discuss answers before giving them to the class. You could even give an example of an answer. Be sure to acknowledge each child's answer somehow, whether you simply thank the child or reword her answer. Allow enough time for discussion so that each child—even the quieter ones—has a chance to participate.

The fact that these students are readers modifies your role as *information giver.* In classes with younger children, you'd be more of a storyteller. You can encourage fourth and fifth graders to take part in the information giving by letting them read. Be sensitive to readers who still feel insecure in their skills. You can offer them titles or short reading parts, while assigning longer portions to more experienced readers. Let children ask and answer their own questions about the story. Be sure you've reviewed the core of the lesson with your students. You might even ask them to paraphrase it in their own words.

You're a *coach* in Step 3 of the Learning Cycle. Here, you'll help your students understand how the lesson content applies to everyday life. Again, learning centers could be used effectively.

See Chapter 2 to learn more about the Natural Learning Cycle.

Structure the classroom for independent exploration. Use table and floor space to "divide" the room—a circle of chairs, a throw rug, a portable chalkboard, even masking tape that sections off a table can designate different learning stations. Offer several activities for this step. Sometimes you can let the children choose one activity to do for the allotted time. Or, you could have small groups rotate to all the activities. Establish expectations for their behavior and then let them explore on their own. One last hint: if you're doing an activity that requires an even number of participants and there are an odd number of students, upper elementary students will generally welcome your participation.

In your role of *encourager* in the final Learning Cycle step, you need to help the children connect the lesson to their lives. You need to both reinforce what they have learned and encourage them to come up with ways they can use their new knowledge. Some children might create a written response, others an interactive task or visual creation as they think creatively about their individual response. As with younger ages, a group brainstorming session could be a good tactic that helps children come up with ideas of their own. Resist the urge to tell the children what they "should" \get out of the lesson. Trust God's Spirit to help them recognize just what they need, and to lead them to their own application.

Upper elementary students are *logical thinkers*. They are focused on *facts*. Their *reasoning and sorting skills* show that they can understand and apply categories. They operate with a focused sense of *"right and wrong" justice* that shows itself through strong opinions and a need to be "right." Their social development has brought them to a place where they enjoy pursuing *common group goals. Membership* is important to them—they have a strong felt need to be part of a group. Their *analytical skills* set fourth and fifth graders apart from their younger counterparts.

Do

Provide opportunities for students to study the Bible and look up verses, references, and passages.

Encourage acceptance of all God's children—vary the seating frequently.

Allow students to come to group consensus about classroom rules.

Provide opportunities for cooperative group work as well as independent study.

Allow students to make choices between activities.

Keep classroom instruction as concrete and experiential as possible.

Don't

Don't tell students all the Bible content as they passively listen.

Don't allow students to sit in cliques or always with the same peers.

Don't present a set of rules to follow and exclude students from having input.

Don't only have students work individually on projects or activities.

Don't have students do the same thing for the whole lesson.

Don't present abstract concepts like "witnessing" without concrete examples and roleplaying practice.

Curriculum
Check

Does your upper elementary curriculum expect the teacher to do most of the talking throughout the lesson, or does it encourage interaction about the Bible and spiritual truths with the students?

Does your upper elementary curriculum dictate social-control rules that are imposed on students without their feedback, or does it encourage your students to create classroom and game rules?

Does your upper elementary curriculum have every student doing the same thing at the same time, or does it offer activity options for the students?

Does your upper elementary curriculum deal with abstract concepts too early or without sufficient concrete examples, or are the instructional activities concrete and experiential?

What three things do you feel best about in your upper elementary class? Why? What idea(s) from this chapter can you try to use in your next session?

Chapter 9

Middle Schoolers (Sixth through Eighth Grades): How to Teach the Rapid Changers

Greg and Pauline have worked together in the Children's Education department of their church for years. They enjoy many aspects of their volunteer responsibilities, but they especially like doing things that help them better understand the developmental learning levels of the children they serve. Their mission: to build a program where children learn God's truth in the most effective ways possible.

This creative pair coordinated an informal "test" and shared the results with us.

We'd been discussing if younger children could understand the true meaning of a proverb or parable. Pauline chose a proverb from Ecclesiastes to try on various ages of the children in our church. (The proverb was "He who digs a pit may fall into it . . ." Ecclesiastes 10:8a.) She asked one child from each of the kindergarten, second, fourth, and sixth grade classes to give an explanation of the proverb's meaning. Here's what she discovered:

Question—
What do you think this Bible verse means?
"He who digs a pit may fall into it."

Answers—
Kindergartner: "If you see a big hole, you could fall in."
Second Grader: "You'd have to be dumb to dig a hole that big by yourself."
Fourth Grader: "How could you fall into a hole if you were already inside the hole digging it?"
Sixth Grader: "If you try to make a trap for somebody else, you'd better be careful that you don't fall into your own trap."

Their survey—admittedly informal—is a great illustration of why sixth graders are being grouped into an emerging class of students known as "middle schoolers."

Middle Schoolers: The Rapid Changers

Growing up is a process full of changes. But nowhere does *change* seem to engage children as much as in the sixth through eighth grades.

Schools usually change. This is the age where a student leaves the security of the school building he's known since kindergarten. *Schedules* change. *Teaching methods* and *teachers* change. Middle schoolers may have to find a new set of friends—a daunting task for the pre-teen.

Middle schoolers would rather be with peers than with parents. Group pressure to conform is at its peak. Being with friends becomes a social priority for these students. Quality time at the mall is usually more important than hanging around at home.

Physical changes abound in middle schoolers—or if they don't, frustration does. In either case, insecurities about physical appearance usually blossom. The maturing of the brain in these years accelerates a student's ability to think.

The whole thinking process changes for a middle schooler. These are the years where thinking in concrete terms slowly shifts to *abstract thinking*. Students are less tied to literal interpretations of language. The positive side is that they're better able to understand proverbs and parables, and make mental connections they wouldn't have made before. (Pauline and Gary's report that opened this chapter is an example of this development.) The downside is that they're apt to become frustrated with learning itself in the period between discovering the limits of concrete thinking and learning how to make abstract thinking work for them.

As they reason more comprehensively, middle schoolers *reflect* about themselves. Too often, they don't like what they see. They can be just as frustrated with their own inconsistencies as the adults around them.

On many fronts, middle schoolers aren't exactly children. But they're not exactly adults either. Being caught "in between" makes these years a challenge for students—and those who teach them.

One of the biggest changes for middle schoolers is their *shift from elementary school to middle school.* Increasingly, this shift is happening at sixth grade. Most administrators consider grouping sixth, seventh, and eighth grades together as "middle schools" to be a better developmental arrangement than "junior highs" that begin at the seventh grade (Valentine, et al, 1993). That trend has taken root in U.S. education. In 1973, there were 2,308 public middle schools and 7,878 public junior high schools. Two decades later, there were 9,573 middle schools compared to 3,970 junior highs (National Center for Education Statistics 1995).

Middle schools are designed to be more flexible than the traditional junior high, which is often meant to be simply a downward extension of high school. Still, the shift from elementary school is a profound change for a student. It usually means a different school building, a new set of friends, a new schedule, and a number of different teachers (Schickedanz, et al, 1990).

Peers are a driving influence during the middle school years. As they strive to "be somebody," middle schoolers look for a place among their peers. Their social life changes radically. Friendships, intimate relationships, and group activities tend to dominate the child's life. Remember the boy who was once content to watch TV at home with his parents on Friday night? Now he wants to be with his buddies at the basketball game. How about the girl who loved running the lemonade stand at the end of her driveway on Saturday mornings in the spring? Now she lives to go to the mall and spend time with her friends (Schickedanz, et al, 1990). And while they're seeking autonomy from their parents and other adults, often they're seeking to conform to their peer groups (Slavin 1994).

Physical changes become apparent in many middle school students as they approach and enter puberty. Girls usually precede boys through the process. But just as impressive are the unseen physical changes in the brain during these years. Between the ages of 11 and 13, both the left and right hemispheres are fully developed. The major bridge between the hemispheres, called the *corpus callosum*, is fully matured. At that point this cerebral bridge carries four billion messages per second across its 200–300 million nerve fibers. The brain is ready for extra challenges—including that of abstract thinking (Jensen 1998).

So the middle schooler is primed for a shift—a gradual shift—from concrete logical thinking to *abstract thinking*. The common element is a new flexibility that allows the student's mind to reach beyond concrete, individual experiences to make connections that were previously unseen.

By the time children are 11 or 12 years old they begin to escape from literal interpretations of language—one aspect of concrete thinking giving way to abstract thinking. This "escape" allows children to understand proverbs and parables (Schickedanz, et al, 1990).

Just as physical changes happen at different ages and rates from child to child, so does the shift from concrete to abstract thinking. Teachers should help middle schoolers explore the uses of abstract thinking, but need to remember that it takes students several years to fully develop their newfound skills (Slavin 1994).

We need to be patient with our middle schoolers while they work through the transition between concrete and abstract thinking.

As the middle schooler begins to discriminate between "facts" and "opinions," he moves into a position called "defended realism." He continues to believe that there is a set of facts about the world. Differences in information can produce disagreements about those facts. That can threaten his established set of facts. The student also recognizes opinions, which can differ due to personal tastes.

Sometimes he encounters someone who views one of his facts as "controversial," and might further threaten his set of facts. The combined "threats" from different information and others' opinions tend to put him in a position of a constant defense of his facts—thus the description "defended realism." The net effect of this process is that his realm of "facts" keeps shrinking and the realm of "opinions" keeps growing (Schickedanz , et al, 1990).

Middle schoolers are becoming *reflective*, too. They think about what's going on in their own minds. They study themselves. They start to realize that their behavior doesn't always match what they think and feel. They are prone to be dissatisfied with themselves, especially as they compare themselves with others. They often try to change the way they are (Slavin 1994).

As noted earlier, there's an overwhelming national trend in education to group sixth graders with seventh and eighth graders. The change is not without reason. Most educators consider the grouping to be best for developmentally appropriate middle level programs. In Christian education, sixth graders have proven to be ready for more in-depth Bible study with discussion, applications to life, and complex issues than younger students. That's why we suggest the sixth-through-eighth-grade grouping be followed in Sunday schools if at all possible. (See Chapter 3 for more information about age grouping.)

Which of these characteristics do you notice most in your class of middle school students?

Teaching to Reach Middle Schoolers

Dealing with change in school buildings, routines, and friends certainly challenges students as they begin middle school. (It also continues to challenge some students through their high school years.) The more you make your classroom into a place of clear boundaries, relationships, and activities that make them feel loved and needed, the more stability your middle school students will sense. They'll begin to see your time with them as a much-needed "safe haven" that can help them deal with the changes going on.

Middle school means *a profound emphasis on peer relationships.* Everything you can do to provide opportunities—with boundaries—for peer interaction will help your classroom time. Consider letting them test ideas with a friend before sharing discussion answers in class. Let them work in small groups or teams when possible.

Physical changes, both visible and internal, mark the middle school years. Here's one area where you must remember that middle schoolers are no longer children, but not yet adults. The insecurities brought on by feelings of early teen "gawkiness" need to be handled with sensitivity. Remind your students that your classroom is a place where everyone matters, and everyone is treated with respect.

Whoso neglects learning in his youth,
Loses the past and is dead for the future. — Euripedes

Learning of all kinds needs to impact middle schoolers, especially because they are reflecting on who they are. The intervention of the Gospel as it comes through in your Sunday school class could be just what is needed to make a student come alive—now and for the future!

The gradual shift from concrete to abstract thinking becomes evident in middle schoolers. With the new flexibility in their thinking, middle schoolers can begin to handle concepts like "grace."

They have a new understanding, and therefore a new appreciation, of proverbs and parables. So talking about ideas and what verses mean helps these students explore abstract thinking.

Keep in mind that sometimes they'll ask awkward questions as they make the shift from concrete to abstract thinking. Remember that just as students

So what does your driver's license say for hair color?

won't develop at an equal pace physically, they also won't develop at an equal pace in their thinking abilities.

Middle school students develop *the ability to reflect on their own thoughts and actions.* They strive for a sense of who they are in the middle of all these changes. You can help them explore roles and new characteristics by using drama in class. It's a safe form of experimentation that encourages them to consider how a certain behaviors match—or don't match—what they think is important (Slavin 1994).

What do you enjoy best about teaching middle schoolers?
What challenges you the most about teaching them?

The Natural Learning Cycle* and Middle School Students

Your role as *motivator* means you need to offer a *context for learning* to your middle schoolers. Discussion works well to help them bring their life experiences from the week into the class. More often than not, an activity like playing the "Twenty Questions Game" will prove to be a helpful tool to "prime the pump" for that discussion. Small group discussion, or discussion in pairs, is advisable to allow greater participation before students share with the whole class. As you discuss, try to maintain good eye contact with your students. Lay down the kind of ground rules that allow your students to share what they think and feel with openness and respect from both you and the rest of the class. Allow enough time for discussion so that each student—even the shy one who seems hesitant to speak up—has a chance to participate.

Your role as *information giver* to middle schoolers often means making sure there are enough copies of printed material to go around. Plan on having enough copies on hand for both regular students and visitors. Be sensitive to readers who lack confidence in their "reading aloud" skills. You can offer them titles or short reading parts, while assigning longer portions to more experienced readers. If a passage involves difficult names, read it to the class yourself. Let students ask their own questions about the story and answer them for each other.

You're a *coach* in Step 3 of the Learning Cycle. Here you'll help your students understand how the lesson content applies to everyday life. Again, activity options could be used effectively. Structure the classroom for independent activities. Leave copies of instructions at each activity location. Be available to clarify those instructions—but remember at this age, students should be able to handle less direct supervision. Use table and floor space to "divide" the room—a circle of chairs, a throw rug, a portable chalkboard, even masking tape that sections off a table can designate different learning stations. Offer several activities for this step. Sometimes you'll want the students to choose one activity to do for the allotted time. Or, you could have small groups rotate to all the activities.

See Chapter 2 to learn more about the Natural Learning Cycle.

Establish expectations for their behavior and then let them explore on their own. Ask the students to share their experiences with the rest of the class before moving on to the next Learning Cycle step.

In your role of *encourager* in the final Learning Cycle step, you can help the middle schoolers connect the lesson to their lives. You'll want to reinforce what they have learned and encourage them to come up with ways they can use their new knowledge. As with younger ages, a group brainstorming session could be a good activity that helps children come up with ideas of their own. Then encourage each student to make a personal choice from the group ideas. Resist the urge to tell your class what they "should" get out of the lesson. Trust God's Spirit to help them recognize just what they need, and to lead them to their own application.

The Ways Middle Schoolers Learn

Change *is the definitive word for a middle schooler. The characteristics of a middle school student (sixth, seventh, or eighth grade) are these:*

(1) *dealing with change in school buildings, routines, and friends;*
(2) *a profound emphasis on peer relationships;*
(3) *physical changes (both visible and internal);*
(4) *a gradual shift from concrete to abstract thinking; and*
(5) *the ability to reflect on one's own thoughts and actions.*

Your efforts to reach your middle school students might be easier if you keep these characteristics in mind.

TAKE 2 *to review*

Change is the definitive word for middle schoolers. They deal with a profound *change in school buildings, routines, and friends* at the outset of these years. *Peer relationships* matter more than ever before. In fact, the pressure to conform to the group will never be greater than between the ages of 11 and 13. *Physical changes* can add to the sense of instability felt by middle schoolers. These changes are not only those commonly recognized as a part of puberty, but also changes in the brain that allow for a *gradual shift from concrete to abstract thinking*. As their reasoning capacities grow, middle schoolers also develop *the ability to reflect on their own thoughts and actions*. They won't always like what they see in themselves. That makes this age an ideal time to keep reinforcing the notions that God really likes them and has a future for them.

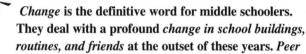

WHAT WORKS WHAT DOESN'T

Do

Allow for plenty of group interaction time, with partners, small groups, or with the whole group.

Create an atmosphere where every student is valued and included—encourage acceptance of all.

Don't

Don't have students only work independently.

Don't allow students to sit in cliques or always with the same peers; don't embarrass students for any reason.

WHAT WORKS   WHAT DOESN'T

Do

Set up opportunities for active games and team activities.

Encourage the exchange of ideas and much discussion—find out what they are thinking.

Allow students to make choices between activities; balance competitive and non-competitive activities.

Pose challenging questions that expand the students' thinking.

Help the students understand the symbolism and truths represented in proverbs and parables.

Encourage students to choose to make a plan to apply what they learned during the week.

Don't

Don't rely on seatwork for the entire class period.

Don't do all the talking and expect students to listen.

Don't have the students do the same thing the whole time.

Don't give students all the answers.

Don't expect every student to fully understand figurative language.

Don't dictate to students how to use what they have learned.

Curriculum
Check

Does your middle school curriculum ask the teacher to simply dispense knowledge, or does it provide opportunities to find out what the students are thinking?

✓ Does your middle school curriculum have every student doing the same thing at the same time, or does it offer activity options for the students?

✓ Does your middle school curriculum assume that the students will understand the symbols in Scripture, or does it give them some help with figurative language?

✓ Does your middle school curriculum dictate how the lesson should be applied, or does it allow for the students to plan their own applications?

What three things do you feel best about in your middle school class? Why? What idea(s) from this chapter will you try to use in your next session?

Chapter 10

High Schoolers (Ninth through Twelfth Grades): How to Teach the Identity Seekers

Where's the "payoff" for teaching teenagers? Many of us who have dealt with teens would agree that for the most part, it takes a few years to feel appreciated for contributing to the development of a teenager into a thriving young adult. But every once in a while, a teacher receives thanks from a person-in-process. A high school Sunday school teacher in Virginia shared this letter he received from a former student:

Dear Mr. Jacobson,

I'm writing today to tell you some things I should have said before my family moved. I was either too scared or too dumb to tell you face-to-face before we had to say good-bye. I'm sorry. I didn't realize how much I learned my freshman and sophomore years that I spent in your Sunday school class. I took you way too much for granted.

Things are a real challenge right now. I'm dealing with some stuff in my life that is really hard. What's going on makes it almost impossible for me to know which decisions I should make or which direction I should go. From the outside it looks like I have to make a choice between two equally important but different paths. Whatever I decide, someone is going to be hurt. Really hurt. Either path could have a huge bearing on the direction that my life takes. I wish I could tell you more. What I can tell you is this: your Sunday school teaching made a huge impact on me.

First, I want to thank you for not judging us like we were "immature teenagers." You were open with us. That helped us discover more about who and what we were. It was really cool. You were more into guiding us to help us find out for ourselves what the Bible says about life. You didn't try to think for us. Even though no one may have ever told you, I think every one of us in your class felt like you were really there to help us succeed with God and in our lives.

Second, you taught me that life doesn't always have storybook endings. You said that was okay, because no matter how it looks, God is still in control of my life if I trust Him and give everything to Him. That's where I'm at right now. I feel scared, but I also know that He will lead me.

I just wanted to let you know that I'm thankful that God let me spend two years in your high school class. You really made a difference for me.

Thanks again,
Melissa

The high school years are filled with critical decisions and big questions. That's why your input can be so important to the teenagers you teach.

High Schoolers: The Identity Seekers

In the high school years—here defined as the ninth through twelfth grades, ages 14 through 18—a person's *identity* is largely established. This is the time when teenagers will examine and challenge values and beliefs. They'll try out roles. They'll spend time with hobbies and habits that could stay with them for their entire lives.

Peers continue to be an extremely important influence. At the high school level, the influence of peers may be less on external appearance than on internal opinions. Opinions and actions of peers matter more than fashion as the high school years unfold. And as a teen's identity becomes more established, he becomes more autonomous and less conformed to a certain group.

Although many experts suggest that high school students have fully entered into *abstract thinking*, practical experience shows that the transition is not complete for a significant number of students. That being said, high school students are still largely ready to tackle more complex thought. Proverbs and parables are well within their understanding. They thrive on discussion and new ideas—if, of course, they want to.

Which of these characteristics do you notice most in your class of high school students?

The search for *identity* is a key characteristic of the high school years. This search is closely tied to a teenager's ability to reason as she experiments with relationship and roles; during this time she'll also be testing her values and beliefs, and how (or whether) to act on them.

The teenager dreams about possibilities. She imagines her future; she sees herself in varied occupational and social roles. In sessions with friends, she sometimes debates moral and spiritual issues: Can participating in a war ever be moral? What rights do people really have? What would an ideal world look like? What does God think about me? (Miller 1989)

The debates—both internal and external—over "big questions" like these are helping her determine the values she will call her own. The "big questions" concern her. But often the questions of personal identity are a greater frustration. Consider this diary entry from a high school student:

What is going to be really important to me? Am I a failure because I didn't get asked out this weekend or because I got a C- on my last exam? Why do I feel like I have no friends, when I know I have so many good ones? Who am I?

When my spiritual life is a mess, my whole life feels like a mess. I know not to measure by the world's standards, but the world is all around me! Where are you, God?

The diary entry shows that even students who seem to "have it all together" struggle to keep a positive focus. They're preparing for adulthood; sometimes they panic because life can seem to be out of control.

This also shows that, even though a high school student is better equipped than ever to consider life and social issues from a number of different perspectives, she still holds on to a certain self-centeredness. She can see how issues impact a larger set of social relationships, but can tend to believe that the sheer force of her logic—or a positive resolution to one of her problems—will move mountains. She is still naive about the practical problems involved in achieving an ideal future for herself (Miller 1989).

But looking to the future is exactly what these years seem to be designed for. The high school years mark the age of the student's introduction into adult society much more than the age of puberty, which generally occurs earlier (Piaget & Inhelder, 1969).

An identity develops in these years that can foreshadow the adult years. A group of eleven year olds will tend to look the same and do the same things. However, six years later, some will be delinquents or drop-outs, while others will become artists, athletes, honor students, or budding mechanics (Slavin 1994).

Peers continue to be a driving influence in the high school years. That's a bothersome thing to many parents and teachers, but a fact nonetheless. Friendships, popularity, conflict with peers, and the prospect of dating all take an enormous amount of a teenager's attention and energy. Even though this is a time when teens try to establish their own personal identities, the actions and opinions of their peers weigh heavily upon them. Fads are shared and rejected as a group. Friendships formed in this

"Dear God, help me to be more considerate of my friends' feelings, even if most of them are WAY too sensitive."

stage of life may endure through life, either in reality or in nostalgia (Slavin 1994).

Parents sometimes worry that their teenage children are so fused with their peer group that instead of establishing an individual identity, they've lost it completely. They could take heart in this: Peer influence is greater in early adolescence. Older teens tend to conform less to their peer groups (Schickedanz, et al, 1990).

The gradual shift into *abstract thinking* continues in the high school years. But that shift is not necessarily complete in terms of reasoning skills. Only 5% of all eleven year olds have developed formal reasoning skills. By age 14, that number is 25%. That percentage only goes up to 50% of the population by adulthood. Still, the brain is *physically* primed for the shift to abstract thinking by age 13 (Jensen 1998).

That makes the possibilities of abstract thinking open to high schoolers. But there is some research to support that intellectual advances in teens cannot be explained by developmental stages, as with younger children. Instead, such advances in adolescence resulted from improvements in memory, attention, knowledge, and problem-solving strategies.

Whether or not some teens have strong abstract thinking skills, most of them can think in terms of hypothetical situations. They can imagine almost any set of circumstances. They can think about abstract ideas.

The high schooler is increasingly capable of interpreting and remembering written texts. These are critical study skills. Developed well, these skills can assure academic achievement. In a research study, third, fifth, seventh, and twelfth graders were asked to rate parts of texts in terms of relevance to a theme. The twelfth graders alone were able to distinguish among totally irrelevant, somewhat irrelevant, somewhat relevant, and very relevant material (Schickedanz, et al, 1990).

Teens can examine and evaluate written material. Abilities like these are crucial to learning, especially to learning the Bible. But moral development is also a concern for the Christian educator.

Children really aren't "wired" to make sophisticated moral judgments until they're adolescents. But moral development in teenagers depends upon far more than biology alone. It requires exposure to moral reasoning and values more advanced than theirs. This critical stage in their development needs a context of interaction with supportive family members, peers, and others. Such exposure can challenge teens to think about their own moral beliefs. This time of examination also exposes them to the morals of their parents and other important adults (Schickedanz, et al, 1990).

High schoolers are capable of developing into mature Christians if they are exposed to values from the Bible in interaction with their parents, family members, peers, and significant adults—including Sunday school teachers and youth ministers. The stronger the correlation between the values of all parts of their lives, the better the learning. A teen has an excellent possibility of absorbing, adopting, and becoming all that it means to be a Christian if these factors are "in sync."

In today's world teens are under incredible pressure to experiment with drugs, alcohol, and sex. They hear from powerful people in their world that the God of the Bible is no longer relevant. Positive moral role models can be hard to come by. Your role as a Sunday school teacher, youth minister, or significant adult in a teenager's life can have more impact than you imagine.

While the pre-adolescent years (roughly ages 13 through 15) are focused on helping students handle some remarkable physical and intellectual changes, the adolescent years (roughly ages 15 through 18) are more dedicated to introducing students to adult society (Piaget & Inhelder 1969). This marked division of purpose between the early teen and later teen years is one of the reasons behind our suggestion to group ninth graders with high schoolers. Another major difference between older and younger adolescents is how they deal with peers. Although peers are critical to both age groups, younger adolescents tend to

The Ways High Schoolers Learn

The following developmental characteristics mark a student's high school years:

(1) the search for, and establishment of, personal identity;
(2) the profound influence of peers; and
(3) the continued shift toward abstract thinking.

These characteristics reflect a maturing process that enables a search for values. Keep that search in mind as you seek to reach the high schoolers you teach.

pressure their peers for conformity while older adolescents tend to respect their peers' different ideas. Further, the more developed thinking skills of older teenagers allow them a new level of critical thinking that might intimidate a younger student in the same classroom. (See Chapter 3 for more information about age grouping.)

The imagination of a boy is healthy, and the mature imagination of a man is healthy; but there is a space of life between, in which the soul is in a ferment, the character undecided, the way of life uncertain, the ambition thick-sighted. **— John Keats**

Consider the Mental Flex above, and talk this over with a friend: How much has changed since Keats made this observation in the early 19th century?

Teaching to Reach High Schoolers

The search and establishment of personal identity emerges as a major task in high school years. Christian education, including Sunday school, can help them own biblical values that will help them build their identities. To work through those vital issues requires an atmosphere of trust in the classroom; in fact, the more you can build an atmosphere of a "safe haven" for their ideas, experiences, and—yes—confusion, the better.

Peer relationships are still crucial to consider in teaching high school students. But, as noted above, there is less pressure to conform in high school than in middle school. Rather, they are ready to respect their peers' ideas and to consider adopting them as their own. Small group activities work well with high schoolers. So does curriculum that encourages group problem solving.

Because the gradual shift into *abstract thinking* continues in high school, you can encourage your students to make their own connections to the truths of the Bible. You can offer those truths and ask your class to consider how they challenge the popular beliefs of the day. You can afford a loose class structure and encourage the students to ask questions and to answer them for each other.

What do you enjoy best about teaching high schoolers? What challenges you the most about teaching them?

The Natural Learning Cycle* and High School Students

Your role as *motivator* means you need to provide a *context for learning.* Talking and interaction help high schoolers bring their life experiences from the week into the class, and give them a vehicle to explore new ideas. Establish ground rules that allow your students to share what they think and feel with openness and respect—from you and the rest of the class. Don't be afraid of silence after you ask questions; sometimes teens need time to gather their thoughts. Allow enough time for discussion so that each student—even the shy one who seems hesitant to speak—has a chance to participate.

Your role as *information giver* to high schoolers often means making sure there are enough copies of printed material to go around. Plan on having enough copies on hand for both regular students and visitors. Allow your students to discuss the material. If there are a number of questions, divide them among several small groups of students to cover the lesson content. (Then encourage the groups to share their responses with the rest of the class.)

You're a *coach* in Step 3 of the Learning Cycle. Here, you'll help your students understand how the lesson content applies to everyday life. Structure the classroom for independent activities and leave copies of instructions at each activity location. You can

See Chapter 2 to learn more about the Natural Learning Cycle.

supervise activities, but you don't need to be as directly involved as with younger students. Use table and floor space to "divide" the room—a circle of chairs, a throw rug, a portable chalkboard, even masking tape that sections off a table can designate different learning stations. Sometimes you'll want the students to choose one activity to do for the allotted time. Or, you could have small groups rotate to all the activities. Ask the students to share their experiences with the rest of the class before moving on to the next Learning Cycle step.

In your role of *encourager* in the final Learning Cycle step, you need to help the high schoolers connect the lesson to their lives. As with younger ages, a group brainstorming session could be a good tactic that helps children come up with ideas of their own. Then encourage each student to make a personal choice from the group ideas. Resist the urge to tell your class what they "should" get out of the lesson. Trust God's Spirit to help them recognize just what they need, and to lead them to their own application.

TAKE 2 to review

High school students are in the process of *searching for and establishing an identity.* This means they wrestle with ideas and values upon which they can build their own lives. It's a wonderful time to offer the eternal truths of the Bible for their consideration against the popular beliefs of the day. *Peer influence* is still important to high schoolers. However, the emphasis shifts somewhat from pressure to conform to the group to consideration of peer opinions and values to adopt as one's own. The shift into *abstract thinking* continues in these years, allowing more complex thinking about ideas, the future, and relationships than before.

Do

Expect your students to challenge values and beliefs. Create a place where questioning is "safe."

Encourage discussion one-on-one, with small groups or as a whole class.

Challenge your students to discover what is important to them.

Set up opportunities for active games and team activities.

Encourage the exchange of ideas and much discussion—find out what they are thinking.

Allow students to make choices between activities.

Don't

Don't discourage "big" questions.

Don't lecture exclusively.

Don't assume all students know what is important.

Don't rely on seatwork for the entire class period.

Don't do all the talking and expect students to only listen.

Don't have students do the same thing for the entire lesson.

WHAT WORKS WHAT DOESN'T

Do

Provide activities to encourage group problem solving.

Expose your students to moral reasoning and biblical values.

Encourage students to choose to make a plan to apply what they learned to their lives.

Be a powerful, positive role model.

Don't

Don't give students all the answers.

Don't hesitate to challenge students to think about their own moral beliefs.

Don't dictate to students how to use what they have learned.

Don't underestimate the impact you're having on students.

Curriculum Check

Does your high school curriculum make it difficult for your students to talk about their doubts, or does it help you create a safe environment for students to ask their tough questions?

✓ Does your high school curriculum expect passive acceptance of the material by your students, or does it encourage them to take ownership of their beliefs?

✓ Does your high school curriculum expect the teacher to do most of the talking, or does it provide ways to find out what the students are thinking?

✓ Does your high school curriculum dictate how the lesson should be applied, or does it allow for the students to plan and implement their own applications?

What three things do you feel best about in your high school class? Why? What idea(s) from this chapter can you try to use in your next session?

Chapter 11

Adults:
How to Teach the
Cocooned Learners

Jerry and Jeannine are in their late 30s. They have one child ready for college, one in middle school, and one in elementary school. They felt indifferent about the local church they'd attended for the first seven years after they'd come to town, so they left. They tried a few other churches, and then started attending a Wednesday night Bible study. They surround themselves with Christian friends, and encourage their children to attend the programs they like best

among the churches in town. "Between the Bible study, Christian radio, and the latest releases at the bookstore, we feel well-fed spiritually," Jeannine remarked.

"And it's a lot easier than dealing with local church politics," Jerry added.

"Cocooning" is a major trend in our society. It is the tendency of people to insulate themselves in their own self-contained world—and it has never been easier to do.

People can have 256 channels beamed into their big-screen TVs. They can have a different ethnic meal delivered each night to their doorsteps. They can use the Internet to instantaneously communicate with people around the world. They can fax or E-mail their work into headquarters from a home office.

They can surround themselves with information and entertainment, but still be very much alone. People can go through Bible studies and devotionals as individuals. Still, there is one essential ingredient to a fulfilled life that they can never get on their own: community. Community is one reason that Sunday school is so important. Most adults—whatever their age—need to feel like they're valued, contributing members in a significant community.

Adult Sunday school is a terrific place for that to happen. Gearing the format around discussion creates a sense of personal bonding that can counteract the prevalent trend toward adult isolation in our modern world.

Physical and mental development are not as overtly dramatic in adults as in childhood and adolescence. But life does not stay static, so the need for a developing faith never ends. Building the class structure and ambiance around Bible study and community will help people break the cocoons that keep too many adults from genuine growth and personal development.

Adults: The Cocooned Learners

There are many descriptions of the processes a person goes through as an adult. But the following characteristics seem to hold throughout adulthood.

Adults bring a *world of experiences* to any learning situation inside or outside the classroom. They have a substantial background to relate to present situations. They are able and often ready to apply what they learn to their everyday lives, provided they find that learning relevant.

"No, I don't think atheists should be able to file insurance claims for acts of God."

Adults tend to enjoy being *active participants* in a learning situation. They want to exercise choice in what they learn. They enjoy sharing their knowledge with others, especially if they sense that it could help someone else. They learn better by being proactive rather than reactive learners.

Adults seek meaningful *interpersonal relationships*. That means they may come to Sunday school as much for the people in it as the material covered. They'll respond well to an environment that encourages friendships. They won't respond well to an atmosphere that stifles response, or a classroom where just a few people dominate.

Adults develop *unique perceptions* that can enrich the lives of others. No one views a situation exactly the same way as another. Much learning can take place when a commonly-held perception is challenged and examined.

Adult learning hinges on taking *action* of some kind. They want to know how to use what they learn. They remember what they do more than what they only hear. Action reinforces what they have learned, and often leads to further questioning and exploration. Thankfully, most adults want to be *lifelong learners*. They are open to learn and grow, especially through the experiences that mark life transitions (becoming parents, job changes, children leaving home, becoming grandparents, the death of a spouse).

In many ways, adults can be the easiest age of students to teach. And because your role as a teacher is more of a "player-coach" than a lecturer, (even though some adult students may consider you to have the "final word" on some issues), you can enjoy learning from those you teach.

Which of these characteristics do you notice most in your class of adult students?

Common Issues

Frequently, adult classes are formed according to general age groupings. Other times, they are structured around life situations and/or events (for example, young marrieds, singles). Many churches group adult classes with both age and situations in mind.

These issues are common to the age groupings listed below. These guidelines are not hard and fast; rather, these are characteristics that generally apply.

Younger adults (ages 20—35) work on resolving their adult identities. They deal with issues of remaining single, getting married, and establishing a household. The development of adult-level relational abilities is an ongoing task, as can be the development of parenting skills. These are also the years when adults determine their primary vocations. If married, some of these students often have to juggle a schedule where both husband and wife are employed. Demands are growing on their time, career, and relationships. They must sense that the topics offered in a Sunday school class are relevant to their life situations.

Middle adults (ages 35—50) are searching for a spiritual dimension in life. They are often concerned about upward mobility in their careers. Frequently, they are dealing with teenage children or aging parents. They are interested in real-life stories and group discussions.

Older adults (ages 50—65) are making crucial preparations to resolve life questions. They're concerned about having enough money for retirement. They are facing health issues that accompany aging. They're often involved in helping their children get started in their adult lives. They question the meaning of their lives to this point, and want to use their time and energy to make life more meaningful if possible.

Senior adults (ages 65 and above) are seeking—and often find—some degree of resolution to life issues. The overwhelming majority of these adults live on a fixed income. They often seek out volunteer opportunities to use their time profitably. They're understandably concerned about staying healthy and active. These adults can be valuable class members; they're able to advise others because of their wisdom and experiences.

Points of change or *transitions* mark adulthood. Such transitions are triggered by ordinary life circumstances but even more by unexpected, often ill-timed, live events. These can be predictable in one sense, but can still cause problems between husbands and wives if one spouse's transition is "out of sync" with the other's. Transitions can be opportunities for growth, if treated as such. The most problematic transitions seem to be (give or take a few years):

Age 30 — This is the time when youthful dreams have to come to grips with reality.

Age 40 — This is the time when one faces the fact that half of life is over.

Age 60 — This is the age when facing retirement becomes a reality.

People do not launch themselves into adulthood with the momentum of their childhood and simply coast along to old age. — Robert J. Havinghurst

Looking at Adults by Generations

Another helpful way to think about adults is to consider how their historical context shapes their outlook. Generation experts Strauss and Howe have outlined four generations of adult North Americans as follows:

The "G.I." Generation (born 1901–1924) is a generation that was shaped largely by the Great Depression of the 1930s and World War II. These include many of our senior citizens today. They are hardy, civic-minded, patriotic optimists. Even so, they can be a bit intolerant and have something of an entitlement mindset. If they are healthy and independent, they are interested in enjoying themselves with their peers and families. They may be faithful church members, but most are not likely to be interested in changing their lifestyles or opinions very much.

The "Silent" Generation (born 1925–1942) was largely too young to go to World War II. They grew up in awe of the preceding generation and consequently adopted their values. Later, they were influenced by the Boomers who followed them. Thus, many in this generation went through significant values changes. However, since not as much was heard from them as from the preceding and succeeding generations, they are often called "silent." They tend to be well-educated, capable, and justice-loving, but can also be inde- cisive and bureaucratic. Silents make up a large portion of many adult Sunday schools and have enough experience to contribute a great deal—but they may like to defer those opportunities to Boomers.

The "Boomer" Generation (born 1943—1960) have exercised a power in American society far out of proportion to their numbers. They caused the social ferment of the 1960s and early 1970s, and were the yuppies of the 1980s. They have mellowed somewhat, but still tend to be brash. They tend to pursue their own spiritual paths, which may or may not involve Christianity. Although heavily involved in family and professional duties, Boomers are often will- ing to take part in church activities and spiritual development—if they can. When involved, they can be a significant force in leading a church into its future. On the downside, Boomers involved in church often expect their needs to be catered to.

The Ways Adults Learn

Adults' lives are marked by:

(1) transitions;
(2) family involvement; and
(3) vocational concerns.

A wide variety of life events impact the adult years.

The more relevant your class can be in making God's Word connect with the lives of your students, the greater impact you'll have.

The "13th" Generation (born 1961—1981) receive their name from being the 13th generation born since the American Revolution. They are also commonly known as *Generation X.* Some unfortunate social circumstances mark these young adults: a weakening economy, permissive parenting, and the breakdown of the family. This backdrop served to make many of them emotionally wounded and pessimistic about the future. But it also forced them to become creatively pragmatic and to form strong friendships to help them get by. They are often called the first "postmodern" generation due to a lack of belief in God or absolutes. "Xers" are often very spiritual, but aren't necessarily Christian. They may be open to the truths of the Bible, but will be better convinced if they can see those truths demonstrated in the lives of Christians. They are highly relational, and expect their teachers to "be real" with them (Strauss & Howe 1998).

So where do you begin in a strategy to group adults together in classes? Usually a Sunday school's adult class groupings are a mix of common ages and common interests. Often a Sunday school will offer a class that can help students transition into adult Sunday school (for example, a College and Career or a Young Marrieds class). Then younger adults will tend to establish classes of their own that, if the members are more permanent than transient, might allow them to stay with most of the same class members throughout adult Sunday school. Other churches will form classes based on personalities. They'll offer a high-energy discussion-based class for those adults who enjoy active discussion, and a more laid-back class for those adults who are more reflective. And there could still be a need for "time of life" classes—specially focused classes for senior adults, young parents, and singles, for example. Of course, there are smaller churches which only offer one adult Sunday school class. The challenge for the teacher of this class is to speak meaningfully to students of all ages and stages of life.

That is what learning is. You suddenly understand something you've understood all your life, but in a new way. — Doris Lessing

Take another look at the above Mental Flex. Can you think of a few examples from your own life that could be used to illustrate it?

Teaching to Reach Adults

Most adults will respond better to your role as a teacher if you enter that role as a peer rather than an authority figure. They'll appreciate the fact that you're a fellow pilgrim who can relate to their struggles and joys through common experience.

Transitions, including family and professional concerns, are events that can trigger both stress and growth in adults. As a teacher, you need to be aware of the kinds of transitions facing your individual class members if at all possible. Don't feel constrained to relate every specific item in your curriculum to those transitions. You should be able to offer enough of a forum in your classroom that they can share comfortably and freely about their own lives at their own discretion.

Cover topics that Christians face at any age (building better relationships, putting God first in your life, finding freedom in Christ). Connect the lesson content with everyday life. Offer a time of reflection and activity that gives the student the opportunity to determine a strategy of personal application of the lesson content during the week.

What do you enjoy best about teaching adults? What challenges you the most about teaching them?

The Natural Learning Cycle* and Adult Students

Your role as *motivator* means you need to provide a *context for learning*. Sometimes a short, attention-getting story that leads into the lesson content is a great tool for engaging your students in the day's session. Discussion is the primary means to actively involve class members in the lesson. You might want to form small discussion groups so a greater number of students will be involved. If your class is small (10 or fewer students), consider treating it as its own small group.

Your role as *information giver* to adults means making sure there are enough copies of printed material to go around. Plan on having enough copies on hand for both regular students and visitors. Allow your students to discuss the material. Ask questions that reveal whether students have grasped the lesson material during this step. In-depth application questions can come later in the lesson.

You're a *coach* in Step 3 of the Learning Cycle. Here, you'll help your students understand how the lesson content applies

See Chapter 2 to learn more about the Natural Learning Cycle.

to everyday life. Although many adults may be used to lecturing as the main means of encountering classroom material, they might welcome some variety. So consider some creative or out-of-the-chairs activities that might help your students make the connection between everyday life and the lesson content.

In your role of *encourager* in the final Learning Cycle step, you need to help the adults connect the lesson to their lives. Here again, an activity could be a great way to help adults make that connection. Don't be afraid to give adult students things to do at home (such as daily Bible readings) to reinforce the lesson content throughout the week.

Adult students continue to be shaped by life experiences, even though the rapid development of childhood and youth may be over. Transitions mark an adult's life with events that can produce both stress and growth. *Family concerns* change throughout adult life, as do *vocational concerns*. Adults respond well to material that easily relates to their life experiences.

WHAT WORKS · WHAT DOESN'T

Do
Create a sense of community.

Don't
Don't provide only individual study opportunities.

Gear the format of your class around discussion and idea exchange.

Don't lecture exclusively.

Help adults see the relevance of what is being learned. Connect the content of the lesson with everyday life.

Don't teach the content and facts without applications.

Provide choices for learning activities.

Don't have the class do the same thing the whole time.

Cover topics that Christians face at any age; understand the differences between adult generations.

Don't underestimate the value of adult generations learning from one another.

Honor the unique learning styles of individual adults.

Don't assume that all adults learn the same.

Offer a time for students to determine a strategy of personal application of the lesson content during the week.

Don't dictate to the students how to use the lesson in their lives.

Curriculum
Check

✓ Does your adult curriculum assume that your students have all had the same experiences, or does it honor the unique experiences of the students and incorporate those events into the lessons?

✓ Does your adult curriculum focus too much on content and not enough on relevant application, or does it present a balance between the two?

✓ Does your adult curriculum favor one generation over another, or does it value intergenerational experiences and dialogue?

✓ Does your adult curriculum dictate how the lesson is to be applied, or does it encourage students to plan and implement their own applications to the lesson?

What three things do you feel best about in your adult class? Why? What idea(s) from this chapter can you use in your next session?

Epilogue

Why Teachers Like You Matter

Do you think you can make a difference as a Sunday school teacher?

Before you answer, let's consider the story of Charles. Charles was a day laborer. He was barely able to read, but he was a man of prayer. His attitude and openness caught the attention of Fred, a brilliant young student who worked for one of Charles' neighbors. Charles asked Fred to join him for a prayer meeting. Before long, Fred became Charles' student on Sundays. Fred helped Charles through words he couldn't read, and Charles taught Fred what he knew about God's Word and being a disciple of Jesus Christ.

Fred was hungry for spiritual truth. He began to spend every spare moment with Charles—so much time, in fact, that his employer threatened to whip Fred if he went to see Charles for religious training apart from Sundays again.

That's right, "whip." Fred's full name was Frederick Douglass—the most prominent black abolitionist of the nineteenth century. He was still a slave when Charles Lawson became his Sunday school teacher and spiritual mentor. He trusted Lawson for advice on one of the toughest issues of human history, and a personal one for Douglass: slavery. In his autobiography, Douglass wrote:

   . . . my chief instructor in religious matters was Uncle Lawson. He was my spiritual father and I loved him intensely. . . . The good old man had told me that the Lord had great work for me to do, and

I must prepare to do it . . . though I could not see how I could ever engage in its performance. The good Lord would bring it to pass in his own good time, he said, and that I must go on reading and studying the Scriptures. This advice and these suggestions were not without their influence on my character and destiny. He fanned my already intense love of knowledge into a flame by assuring me that I was to be a useful man in the world. When I would say to him, "How can these things be? and "What can I do?" his simple reply was, "Trust in the Lord." When I would tell him, "I am a slave, and a slave for life, how can I do anything?" he would quietly answer, "The Lord can make you free, my dear; all things are possible with Him; only have faith in God. 'Ask, and it shall be given you.' If you want liberty, ask the Lord for it in faith, and He will give it to you."

Thus assured and thus cheered on under the inspiration of hope, I worked and prayed with a light heart, believing that my life was under the guidance of a wisdom higher than my own. With all other blessings sought at the mercy seat, I always prayed that God would, and in His own good time, deliver me from my bondage . . . (Douglass 1882).

Frederick Douglass went on to help transform a nation as a free man—not only under the law of the land, but in Christ Jesus. He credited Charles Lawson as being one of his most significant mentors throughout his life. Lawson was responsible for nurturing Frederick Douglass in the Word and ways of God—and history was changed because of his efforts.

In the same way, you're responsible to nurture your students in the Word and ways of God. Who knows how that might impact the history of a nation? Just as important, who knows how your efforts might impact the life of one of your students this week!

How God Can Use You in the Lives of Your Students

The roles you take on through your class sessions are also descriptions of the roles you can play in your students' lives.

You can be a *motivator* to your students. You can help them to their next level of spiritual development. Because you are in a unique position of trust with your students, you could even provide the support they need to take risks that can help them grow.

You also function as an *information giver* in the lives of your students. There are facts you offer that they may not get anywhere else. And you may be surprised how much they use what you offer.

You can also be a *coach* for your students. You can suggest, or even provide, ways for them to practice their faith.

You can also be an *encourager* to your students. Like few others, you can cheer them on to apply their faith in day-to-day life.

The very fact that you are a teacher makes you an influence in the lives of your students. God can take that influence and use it to change their lives.

Teachers Like You

Have you gone through some valleys as a Sunday school teacher? If so, we pray that God will use this book to help you back up the mountain. As you've read this book, you've reviewed many ideas that can help you reach every student you teach. You've discovered practical ways to match the developmental levels of your students. You've learned to implement classroom strategies that address the learning styles of your students through the Natural Learning Cycle.

You'll pick and choose the right things for your students, because you know them better as a group than anybody else. You'll continue to change lives by adjusting what you can to help your students learn better.

No book, no "new" idea, no seminar can replace *you*. You have students who count on you week in and week out to lead them that much closer to the truth of God's Word.

You're already a teacher. God is already using you.

You're making a difference. You may see the difference this week, or you may wait for years to notice it. But make no mistake: teachers like you matter.

They always have. They always will.

A teacher affects eternity; he can never tell where his influence stops. — **Henry Adams**

Bibliography

Ames, L. B.; Gillespie, C.; Haines, J.; and Frances, L. *Evaluating the Behavior of the Preschool Child.* New York: Harper & Row, 1979.

Douglass, Frederick. *Life and Times of Frederick Douglass: from 1817—1821. Written by Himself.* Christian Age Office, 1882.

Englebretson, Rosann; Hiebert, E.; and Juel, C. *Ready Readers.* Parsippany, NJ: Modern Curriculum Press, 1997.

Jensen, Eric. *Teaching with the Brain in Mind.* Alexandria, VA: ASCD, 1998.

Kegan, Robert. (1982). *The Evolving Self.* Cambridge, MA: Harvard University Press, 1982.

Kennedy, William Bean. "Christian Education Through History." *An Introduction to Christian Education.* edited by Marvin J. Taylor. Nashville: Abingdon Press, 1966.

Kotulak, Ronald. *Inside the Brain.* Kansas City, MO: Universal Press, 1996.

LeFever, Marlene. *Learning Styles: Reaching Everyone God Gave You to Teach.* Colorado Springs, CO: David C. Cook Publishing Co., 1994.

————. *Creative Teaching Methods.* Colorado Springs, CO: David C. Cook Publishing Co., 1996.

McEwin, C. K.; Dickinson, T. S.; and Jenkins, D. *The Professional Preparation of Middle Level Teachers.* Columbus, OH: National Middle School Association, 1995.

Miller, Patricia H. *Theories of Developmental Psychology.*
New York: Freeman & Co., 1989.

National Center for Education Statistics. *Digest of Education Statistics.* Washington D.C., 1995.

Piaget, Jean; Inhelder, Barbel. *The Psychology of the Child.*
Basic Books, 1969.

Routman, R. *Invitations.* Portsmouth, NH: Heinemann, 1991.

Schickedanz, J. A.; Schickedanz, D. I.; Hansen, K.; and Forsyth, P. D. *Understanding Children.* Mountain View, CA: Mayfield, 1990.

Shinn, Roger L. "The Educational Ministry of the Church." *An Introduction to Christian Education*, edited by Marvin J. Taylor. Nashville: Abingdon Press, 1966.

Shore, Rima. *Rethinking the Brain: New Insights into Early Development.* New York: Families and Work Institute, 1997.

Slavin, Robert E. *Educational Psychology.* Needham Heights, MA: Allyn and Bacon, 1994.

Strauss, William, and Howe, Neil. *The Fourth Turning.*
New York: Broadway Books, 1998.

Valentine, J. W.; Clark D.; Irvin J.; Keefe, J.; and Melton, G. *Leadership in Middle Level Education.* Vol. 1. *A National Survey of Middle Level Leaders and Schools.* Reston, VA: National Association of Secondary School Principals, 1993.

Video: *Reach Every One You Teach.* Colorado Springs, CO: David C. Cook Ministries, 1998.

Appendix

The Natural Learning Cycle in Action

Hey, kids.
Tell us something important about you!

melissa — I love to talk and make friends.

jason — I'm smart enough to get all A's.

steven — I get into trouble if class isn't fun. I just come up with stuff for me and my friends to do — crazy, fun stuff.

heather — I hate sitting still and learning. Sitting makes me itch.

God has created us so that we learn best when we follow the Natural Learning Cycle.

Link to Last Week's Learning Cycle

"Melissa, did you have a chance to show kindness to someone who was lonely this week?"

"Yes, I saw Allie sitting by herself at lunch and she looked really sad. When I asked to eat with her, her eyes got real big and she said yes!"

Before the Natural Learning Cycle for this week begins, students can talk about how they lived what they learned the week before.

Step 1 of the Natural Learning Cycle

Goal: Capture their attention. Focus their interest.

Key Student Question: Why do I need to know this stuff?

The teacher's role changes in each step of the Natural Learning Cycle.

Teacher's Role: Motivator

In Step 1 of the Natural Learning Cycle, the teacher motivates students, gets them talking, experiencing, and sharing.

Step 1 is Melissa's favorite part of the lesson! She's great at getting the rest of the children to talk about what happened to them during the past week, and she has no trouble talking herself. She's a little lightning rod that draws the class together and sparks interest in the subject. Everyone participates, but this is Melissa's favorite part of the Natural Learning Cycle.

Students like Melissa are often called *Imaginative Learners*.

The wise teacher knows that some of the students in her class will learn in different ways than she does.

So, she doesn't focus on only one or two steps in the Natural Learning Cycle, but encourages students to complete the whole cycle.

This first step of the Natural Learning Cycle is filled with controlled noise—noise that is fun and designed to help everyone answer the question, "Why do I need to study this?"

What methods do students use to help them answer the question *Why do I need to know this stuff?*

- Talking about events during the week
- Playing a team game
- Roleplaying and discussing
- Interviewing each other
- And lots more ways. Every week is different.

When students know that their unique ways of learning will be affirmed—that is, their special places on the Natural Learning Cycle—they enthusiastically participate in the whole lesson. The Natural Learning Cycle honors every child, teen, and adult.

Step 2 of the Natural Learning Cycle

Goal: Learn the facts.

Key Student Question: What do I need to know from the Bible?

Teacher's Role: Information Giver
In the second step of the Natural Learning Cycle the teacher makes sure students know what the Bible says. The teacher will sometimes share what students need to know. Sometimes she will teach students how to study for themselves, at their own age level, in ways that stretch them.

Step 2 is Jason's favorite part of the lesson! He's great at reading. He loves to write.

Students like Jason are often called *Analytic Learners.*

*The wise teacher knows that there is
more than one kind of smart.*

About 30 percent of our students are like Jason.
What about the other 70 percent?

They have equally divided
preferences
across the other
three steps in the
Natural Learning
Cycle. For example,
Melissa's very smart
too. She puts
together what
she's heard in class with what
happened to her last week. She makes everyone feel welcome.
She's smart with people skills.

What methods do students use to help them answer the
question *What do I need to know from the Bible?*

- Listening to a Bible story
- Acting out the story
- Studying verses in pairs
- And lots more ways. Every week is different.

*During Step 2 of the Natural Learning Cycle,
the Sunday school space often looks like a traditional
classroom, with students checking their Bibles and
writing what they discover. By the time this step is over,
everyone will have answered the question,
"What do I need to know from the Bible?"*

Step 3 of the Natural Learning Cycle

Goal: Practice how what was learned could be used this week.

Key Student Questions: How does it work? How might what I found in the Bible get practiced today?

Teacher's Role: Coach
In the third step of the Natural Learning Cycle, the teacher coaches the students to practice, practice, practice. This is the important step where students test how valuable the Bible study is to them.

Step 3 is Heather's favorite part of the lesson! In the classroom laboratory, she gets to be physically active. She needs to move as part of the learning process.
Everyone participates, but this is Heather's most comfortable part of the Natural Learning Cycle. It's filled with focused activity, children moving and talking and learning.

Students like Heather are often called *Common Sense Learners.*

The wise teacher does not stop after Step 2. She does not assume that if students know what the Bible teaches, they will obey it. Sometimes that happens. But more often, children don't know how to jump from knowing facts to using those facts.

Teens and adults may be able to see how to use what God's Word teaches, but unless they are challenged to apply God's Word to their lives, they simply become Bible-facts smart. And facts alone do not make growing Christians.

What methods do students use to help them answer the questions *How does it work?* and *How might what I found in the Bible get practiced today?*

- Turning the classroom into a practice laboratory
- Doing an art project that reminds students of how to use Bible truth
- Building a model of what was learned
- Taking a self-evaluation quiz
- And lots more ways. Every week is different.

Students who learn best in this part of the Natural Learning Cycle explain it this way. "I get to move. My mind works best when my body is moving. But I don't want to just jump around. I want to move while I'm really learning. I don't want to just learn facts, either. That makes no sense to me. It's not the way my mind works. I want everything I learn in Sunday school to be useful to me during the week, to make sense.

Step 4 of the Natural Learning Cycle

Goal: Creatively plan to do something special for Jesus this week, and then carry out that plan.

Key Student Questions: What can this become? "What, with Jesus' help, can I really do for Him with what I learned in class?"

Teacher's Role: Encourager
In the fourth step of the Natural Learning Cycle, the teacher encourages students to take action for Jesus during the week.

Step 4 is Steven's favorite part of the lesson! Steven has lots of ideas. He can think of more ways for him and his friends to live for Jesus than any other student in the class. Everyone participates, but Steven acts as point person. He's the student leader.

Students like Steven are often called *Dynamic Learners*.

A wise teacher affirms the good ideas and helps the class change those that might not be so good. She doesn't always insist on the class doing her idea. Students like Steven need to see their ideas in action, too.

What methods do students use to help them answer the questions *What can this become?* and *"What, with Jesus' help, can I really do for Him with what I learned in class?"*

- Brainstorming possible ideas
- Making a reminder to display at home
- Praying for specific requests
- Setting up accountability pairs to complete a project
- And lots more ways. Every week is different

Another successful Sunday. It was a great start.

But the real successes will come during the week. We may not know how much God used this lesson until Melissa, Jason, Heather, and Steven return next Sunday to report on what they did for Jesus.